THE WHOLE TRUTH AND NOTHING BUT THE TRUTH

By Rory Macdonald

Prologue By David Headley

1ST CHOICE CHRISTIAN PUBLISHING

THE WHOLE TRUTH AND
AND NOTHING BUT THE TRUTH
Copyright © 1st Choice Christian Publishing
19th March 2010

All Rights Reserved

ISBN 978-0-9565397-0-0

First Published 1ST April 2010 by
1st Choice Christian Publishing, 158 St. John's Road,
Corstorphine, Edinburgh, Scotland, EH12 8AY

Printed in Great Britain by
www.direct-pod.com

THE WHOLE TRUTH AND NOTHING BUT THE TRUTH

To an ever-present friend in times of need.

CONTENTS

INTRODUCTION

We love stories of love, of loss, of action, adventure, heart-break and redemption. We love stories of justice, of compassion and of kind hearts – of people who take chances and live life differently in radical ways which change the lives of others. This is one of those stories. Unlike many of the stories you hear like that though, this one is entirely true. There is not one word of fiction in this book. To be honest though, fiction couldn't dream this up.

CHAPTER 1

Anger consumed David. It was irrational, but the switch had been flicked. At 20-years old this man found himself in prison for attempted murder. And now pacing his cell in Glenochil, a mere 9' by 4', a frenzied desire for blood ate him up once more.

All it had taken was a throw away comment from an unknown inmate. Who was he? That didn't matter. What had he said? That didn't matter either.

The blade was all that mattered. David had to get a blade. It was time to mess this guy up. It didn't even matter so much to get the right guy. Any man would do.

Only in his cloud of red mist did this make any sense. All that mattered to David Headley in that moment was making somebody suffer.

CHAPTER 2

The sign on the fire alarm said 'Break glass'.

What else was six-year old David supposed to do?

Standing there in the school corridor whilst everyone else sat in class, it seemed like a fairly straight forward instruction. Ok, so there was no fire but the sign said just break the glass. Yes, it would set off the alarm. Yes, panic would ensue. But it would be funny. It seemed too good to be true.

He stared at the words again. Break. Glass.

Simple.

David clutched a chunk of clay in his hand and almost salivated as excitement and fear intermingled in his mind, setting his stomach buzzing with frenzied butterflies.

Break. Glass.

He looked down at his hand once more and checked both ways down corridor to see if anyone was watching.

All clear.

He raised his hand and project the clay forwards.

The glass was broken.

The school was evacuated. Outside in the playground, hundreds of children poured out in lines, some panic-ing, others simply beside themselves at the thought the school might be burning down. Flustered teachers raced around with registers, trying to account for every child. It was a false alarm though, an act of simple vandalism. To the culprit, it was just a game - a temptation that called out to him louder than common sense.

It wasn't long until he was traced. It hadn't been hard to work out that the mischievous-looking primary two pupil, seen near the fire alarm with a lump of clay moments earlier, had featured heavily in it being set off. He may not have been spotted doing the deed, but the evidence was piled against him anyway.

Later that day, David Headley had his first encounter with the police.

David was so young at the time though that all he got was a slap on the wrists. His family weren't quite sure what to make of his behaviour. Even before this incident, he had a record of causing trouble.

At four-years old, he had caused havoc in Sheffield department store by shutting off the power to the escalator. The switch was supposed to be concealed, but David was inquisitive enough to find it. He deemed any button that could be pushed, to be a button that most certainly should be pushed.

The same went for keys that could be turned. Aged-five he snuck into a Land Rover belonging to his mother's friend that had been parked in the driveway of his home. The family home sat atop a steep hill on Crimicar Drive, in a thoroughly middle-class suburban area of Sheffield. As the lady sat and ate lunch in the house with David's mum, he was setting about opening the door and popping himself in behind the wheel of the vehicle. Once there he turned the keys in the ignition and brought the engine to life with a furious roar. His mum and her friend were drawn from the house by the noise. Had it not been for his inability to operate the hand break, the story may well have ended here.

But here he was at six-years old in trouble with the police. It was a step further than anything they'd encountered before and to his parents his behaviour made no sense - here was a boy being raised in middle-class home with Mum and Dad both present and an older brother that was no trouble at all. They were Methodist church goers - three times on a Sunday - and David was in Sunday school. There was nothing on the face of it to offer any reason for David to act in such a way.

It took just a few months for him to be reacquainted with the Sheffield's police force. Having been at a birthday party for his friend Stevie - a boy of his age that lived just down the road - he decided to take a route home through the Bowl hills, an area renowned to locals as a hang-out for rough necks. It was an area of hilly-wasteland with a reputation as a place where frequenters would whittle away evenings drinking and getting up to no good. It was no place for a six year old boy to be wandering, especially at night. It was in fact a place where children were warned against going, even in the daylight.

But as David wandered through that evening he was completely unfazed by the failing light, the unruliness of his surroundings or the Bowl Hills' intimidating reputation. Whether he was just ignorant of these things or not, he saw nothing to fear. All he saw was adventure however that was not a point of view shared by his parents.

It had still been light when Stevie's mother Judy had taken David to the garden gate and instructed him to walk straight home up the hill to his house. She had no reason to believe he would have done anything other than that - the Headley's house was only 150 yards away and was visible from the gate. But as she sent David on his way and turned back into the house to clear up from the party, David snuck off from the intended route.

A few hours later Judy's phone rang. It was David's mum on the other end of the phone, concerned that that party was going on awful late.

"No, no," said Judy. "I sent David off home up the hill a few hours ago." Outside darkness had set in.

Panic gripped the Headley household and the police were called to report their missing son. A search ensued.

The police found David still in the Bowl hills. He was delivered home to parents, who were pale with worry, in a police car. His face was red from fits of laughter. Unlike everybody else, David thought it was hilarious to be brought home in a police car. His family were just delighted to have him home safe and well.

The Headley family moved to Inverness in the north of Scotland a few years later. David's dad (also called David) needed to move north because of his work. David senior worked in the welding business and got a new job providing and installing equipment to the offshore industry, so they moved up to be closer to the booming north sea oil fields. They had a nice house - four bed rooms with a porch and a garage in a street of nine other houses. It was a solid middle class life. There was always food on the table, all practical needs were met and it was a life of no major dramas and stresses. At least it would have been if it wasn't for David. He was a drama. He was a stress. He was the antithesis of his older brother Jerry.

Jerry held four and a half years over his brother. He was the intelligent, quiet and studious type. David was similarly intelligent but had a brash, boisterous nature which grew bigger as he grew bigger and older. Jerry was of a more settled inkling and never found himself in trouble. David got into enough trouble for both. Mum was always asking of her younger son, "why can't you be more like Jerry?" It made David's teeth grind. It irked him and made him want to be less like Jerry - he wanted to stand out from his older brother.

For the most part though, David and Jerry did their own thing. They stuck to their own circles of friends and didn't spend much time together outside of the house. Jerry was often oblivious to the things David was getting up to. Their relationship worked because they shared a mutual desire to stay out of each others' way.

David always won arguments when the two boys fought. Getting the last word in was of absolute importance. Throughout their childhood Jerry never once beat David up, and their physical battles amounted to no more than a few wrestling matches. Mostly it was verbal and both boys could bite.

For Jerry though it just wasn't worth the hassle of annoying David. When he was nine, Jerry, thirteen at the time, was building a model Lancaster bomber. Having managed to annoy David in some capacity, he then found his model being set on fire and thrown out the window, with David reasoning "It's more realistic."

Despite all this though, few people seemed to hold any lasting grudge against the young boy's behaviour. He carried it all off with a perky, cheeky-chappy charm. He was disruptive though, of that there was no doubt, and day by day the level of worry and distrust his parents felt for him grew. His mum later reasoned that he was just very inquisitive - the polite way of saying he couldn't keep his hands out of trouble. Typically most people could see the funny side of what he got up to, helped probably by David's jovial attitude to everything. He did have a short fuse at times, but overall he viewed most things as a bit of fun. There was no major thought process going on, just a simple equation: if there is potentially a wee kick to be had from it, then do it. Simple. There were no real limitations for him.

In Inverness, David was enrolled in Holm Primary School. It was a brand new, modern school set atop a hill with 120 steps running upto the front door. It was so middle class that even something as small as a teacher being off sick was a big deal.

The game that all ten- year old boys were playing in the playground at that time was Starsky and Hutch. Boys ran around using their fingers as guns making a range of gun noises to add to the fake violence and drama of the game, just like they saw on TV. Some would use just their thumb and forefinger to form the gun others would also include their middle finger to make their imaginary armoury more robust. Sometimes kids would have to put both hands together for greater stability and accuracy when shooting. Of course, that was all make believe. David found make believe to be boring and introduced an air pistol to the game.

He shot three children in the body, just like he saw on TV. The police were called when one of the three of complained, and the gun was discovered in David's schoolbag. For the police to come to this school for something other than road safety sessions was absolutely

14

unheard of. It wasn't an act of malice though, he just believed that a real gun would add realism to the game and make it more fun for the people getting chased.

The gun incident landed David in front of a Children's Panel for the first time. It certainly wasn't to be the last. There he was assessed by a range of psychiatrists and psychologists before being presented with a two year supervision order - essentially probation for those under sixteen years old. He violated the order so frequently it was eventually scrapped.

From then on David became the only child at Holm Primary school to get the belt. His behaviour became so unpredictable that the headmaster, according to David's mum, soon became scared of David. In truth though, it was more likely he feared what David would do next, rather than David himself.

To assume he spent all of his time running around causing mayhem would not do David any justice. He wasn't some sort of loner kid that cut himself off by causing trouble; people knew him and liked him. He had a sense of danger that many young boys have; a need to take risks and feel that rush of excitement.

The neighbourhood children had a game they all played together, whereby they would sneak into a local garden to steal fruit. This garden belonged to an elderly man, infamous to local children, known to as The Colonel.

The Colonel would set trip wires in his garden in a vain attempt to stop children getting at the fruit. He also had a shot gun to act as a deterrent. But these measures had quite the opposite effect to what he was hoping for. Instead of scaring kids away, they added to the rush of stealing his fruit and made it more of a challenge and more of a risk to go in.

Most wouldn't have bothered stealing his fruit if he made it easy, but the Colonel had simultaneously raised the fun factor as he raised the security.

Children would sneak through the woods which surrounded his garden and roll down the hill slope into it to avoid detection. Because the access point to the garden was up a small hill it was easy to be spotted coming in so great lengths were taking to stay under cover. Some would cover themselves with tree branches others would army crawl through the mud. David would go with the neighbourhood kids to raid the Colonel's fruit stocks.

David stuck out from the other children though, not just because of his wild streak. He also looked mature beyond his years. He was ten-years old and 5'8". He was frequently taken for being older, and that made it easy for him to buy cigarettes when he started smoking. His mature looks gave him clout to carry the authority of an adult when he wanted to.

He used that clout to his advantage.

Still aged ten, he started a business to fund his smoking habit. He started a 'roll round', whereby he went round door to door signing up houses to get morning rolls delivered daily. Around 40 homes signed up and so he took on a member of staff - Yvonne Cruikshank, a girl five years his senior. It was her job to share in delivering the rolls to the houses.

The rolls were supplied by a local baker with whom David had negotiated a contract. The deal he brokered was that he would buy the rolls for 12p a dozen and sell them on for 25p per dozen. The original quote from the bakery had been for 15p per dozen, but David told them he had a counter offer from another bakery in order to lower the quote. In truth, there was no other bakery but he kept his bottle and ended up with a good deal. David always kept half the profits, and paid Yvonne 7p a delivery.

His smoking habit wasn't always funded by means so admirable however. He would also sneak into his parent's bedroom and take the loose change his dad left by his bedside, and eventually he took to stealing the family's finest silverware and gold medals given to his father through work. These were sold on. He always complained that he didn't get enough pocket money.

His parents tried everything to get him to settle down. They gave him more pocket money, they tried to persuade him to cut his smoking down - he was by this point a chain-smoker whilst still in primary school.

His thefts weren't all for monetary gain though. Shortly after their move to Inverness, he stole his mother's engagement ring and his grandmother's engagement ring from a dresser in his parents' room to give to his girlfriend at school. Her name was Susan, and that day she became the proud possessor of two diamond rings, despite being only 10-years old.

The whole experience caused David's mum much anguish, as she spent the day at work thinking she had lost them at work. It was fortunate that when Susan's parents found the rings they returned them straight away.

****

David was ten the first time he ran away. He skipped out of school and jumped on the train to Aviemore. It was a trip he had planned in secret and so he had taken the precaution of disconnecting the phone line in his house so the school couldn't phone his parents. By simply snipping the wire he was free to go uninhibited on the short train journey into the scenic surrounds of the Scottish Highlands. He almost made it home in time for tea, but his parents knew he'd been up to something anyway - it was them, after all, that had to foot the hefty bill to have the phone re-connected.

The first time David ran away from home and stayed away he was eleven. He once again utilised the maturity of his looks to try and persuade people he was older than he was. Prior to running away his parents would find reams of tracing paper where he had been practicing forging the signature from the back of his dad's credit card.

He would book himself into hotels with his dad's credit card details and tell the staff that he was 18-years old, that he worked in welding and that he would pay up at the end of the week.

The first time he wasn't so smooth and his immature behaviour made the hotel owner suspicious. David was then over heard on the phone to one of his school friends bragging about how he had skipped off school that day and was now staying in a nice hotel on the other side of Inverness. The owner waited for him to go out for a walk and went into his room where he found David's school bag. David came back from his walk completely unaware that he had been found out, and completely unaware that the hotel owner had called his dad.

David learned the lessons of that first experience and soon perfected his act. After being found out first time, he no longer phoned friends to brag or did anything in the hotel to rouse suspicion. He would simply stick to his story, treat himself to expensive meals, cigars and cider - what he saw to be posh stuff - and leave before the end of the week without paying.

The frustration of his parents grew. His dad would often have to spend time off-shore or down in England as a result of work, and so his mum concluded David junior just wanted to be like his dad.

One night after he had been returned home, David overheard his parents arguing over whose genes he had. Dad claimed their son had inherited his bad streak from the maternal side. Mum countered that the bad genes were almost certainly paternal because someone from David senior's side of the family had attended their wedding without wearing a tie.

Young David built up a record of running away quite quickly, and social workers soon became involved. His parents told the social worker that he was out of control because he kept running away and booking into hotels all around Inverness. At this point he never strayed from Inverness when he ran. Yes, he liked his independence but it was important to stay just close enough to home - he was just a young boy after all.

Often it would take a while for David's family to realise that he had run away. A friend of David's lived up by Loch Ness, and he would often go there to stay. Other times he would just say he was going to stay with his friend and he would skip off to hotels.

The truth is that normality was stressful for David. Home was often not very happy, but to run away meant he could escape the stress, he could even replace the stress with a rush of excitement. It was a vicious cycle though - each time he ran, the home tension grew. In turn that meant every time he came home, he had even more of a reason to run away again.

David running away became almost matter of frequency, to the point where, although his parents would never be free of worry when their son went missing, they did become gradually less surprised when it did happen.

Despite having a life of adventure and drama, David still perceived his parents to be strict. All the other children were allowed to stay out later than he was. It didn't seem fair.

Running away on foot though was begin to fail to suffice. What was needed to really escape was more power, more speed, more thrills. David was setting his sights on getting some wheels.

CHAPTER 3

David had never driven a truck before. At just 12-years old, that was hardly a surprise. He had driven other vehicles though, but this was by far the largest. It was 7.5 ton truck, and David had not accrued it by honourable means. He had stolen it from a car hire business on Market Street in Aberdeen.

The dealership sat on the corner where Aberdeen city centre sank into the rougher surrounds of the harbour area. It was dark and the bustle of daytime activity was fading, being replaced by the night time chorus of drunkards and seagulls echoing between the tall, cold granite buildings. It was no place for a young boy to be alone, but then neither was the driving seat of a truck.

In behind the wheel of the truck David scrambled around. Getting into his vehicle of choice had been a success, but now he realised he was unsure exactly what he was doing. He knew enough to make it move though, and that was all he needed for now.

The truck moved out of showroom onto the streets of Aberdeen. The engine rumbled, it almost seemed too noisy. David needed a plan, but like many of his endeavours he didn't have one. He'd just make it up as he went. For now, all that mattered was getting out of Aberdeen. That was the first objective, but beyond that he had no intended destination.

David had started visiting Aberdeen in the previous year. He was eleven at first and arrived there by accident after boarding the wrong train. By this time he had developed a strategy - that he could do anything as long as he looked like he should be there. He would often board trains and head straight to the first class carriage, where he would fall asleep. He didn't necessarily know where each train was bound for, but he would hop on anyway and fall asleep. No one ever questioned him or asked him for a ticket. That was exactly how he ended up in the Granite City.

He employed this same principal the first time he stole a car - as long as he looked like he should be there, then no one would question him. The car was a Ford Granada, and it was taken from a rental car showroom on Chapel Street in the centre of Aberdeen. The Granada just happened to be the easiest vehicle to get out of the showroom on this occasion - its selection from the available fleet was based on nothing more than this logic.

The area it was in was heavily residential, so it was crucial to not look suspicious. David would wander around the showroom as coolly as possible. When he was sure the coast was clear he set to work breaking the frame off one of the showroom windows. Having done that he was able to lift the pane of glass out and make a silent, trouble-free entry. He would then get behind the wheel of the car and drive it off.

This was part of the charm of Aberdeen to David - he was completely unknown there. Had he been attempting the same things in Inverness - a much smaller town - his chances of getting caught would have been much higher. But Aberdeen was the big city. It was easier to remain anonymous there. There was also much more to do. Aberdeen offered new levels of adventure that Inverness couldn't match.

He didn't get far in the Granada. The police pulled him over at Inverbervie - a small town just south of Aberdeen - because he hadn't paid when he filled up at a service station. It was only after they'd arrested him that they realised the car was stolen too.

The truck moved out of Aberdeen to the south. Adrenaline pumped through David's veins, as the thrill of the steal still set every cell in his body alight. It was a rush. Here he now was in the biggest vehicle he's ever driven bound for the motor way.

By now he'd established a direction - to head for Edinburgh first. From there he planned to see how far the fuel would carry him. He got onto the busy main road south and began to settle down. Passing signs for Stonehaven, his racing heart slowed. He was on his way now, he was clear of Aberdeen. Now he could enjoy the drive.

Midway to Edinburgh flashing blue lights appeared in his rear-view mirror. It was the Police. They signalled to David to pull over, so he obliged.

He rolled down the window as the officer approached.

"How are you doing this evening, sir? Everything well?" the officer asked as he drew up to the truck.

"Yes. All is well here officer," David responded.

The policeman paused and took a good look at David, assessing him.

"How old are you, sir?"

"I'm nineteen," David replied without hesitation. A story well practiced from the hotels.

"Do you have your license and registration documents there?"

David stayed cool and unflustered. "I'm afraid I don't. I just rented this truck to help a friend move house."

The officer paused again, and squinted at David. Inside, the twelve-year old could feel his heart pounding in his chest. The game must surely be up. On the outside though, he didn't flinch. The officer's pause felt like an eternity. In reality, it may just have been a few seconds.

Drizzle fell on the roadside, as the light failed. Eventually the silence broke. "Ok, just be sure to carry your license with you in future," the officer stated firmly.

With that the officer turned and walked back to his vehicle.

David kept cool until the policeman had driven off, then erupted with excitement and disbelief in the truck's cabin. How had he pulled that one off? How had he just convinced a policeman he was nineteen and legally driving a hired truck, when in reality he was twelve and driving a stolen truck? It was too much. What a thrill. What a rush. It beat school and normality any day.

The excitement wore off once more as the road to Edinburgh extended before him. Before long he'd reached the Scottish capital and there he just decided to keep on going. It was late, but he didn't feel like stopping. There was still fuel in the tank, so he was as well to keep moving.

Soon he passed into the Scottish borders, and his eyes were getting heavy. The headlight's piercing the darkness ahead of him put a strain on the eyes.

David woke up as the truck left the road. In a split second, he'd dropped off at the wheel and was now careering up the roadside embankment. Panic wiped out his grogginess and he scrambled to regain control of the truck. He grabbed the steering wheel and bumped the truck back down onto the road. No damage done. Adrenaline once again surged through him. Now he was awake again.

For the rest of the drive his knuckles were white as he gripped the steering wheel of the truck, and his eyes stung as he held them as wide open as he could. He didn't want to leave the road again.

The truck moved further south, over the border into England. David finally stopped when he ran out of fuel near Durham. Normally in these circumstances he would re-fuel and then drive off without paying. It was too difficult to do that here though - the truck was too big, too obvious and too slow off the mark to make a getaway. He opted instead to park up and book into a hotel at Scotch Corner services, just off the motorway in north-east England.

In the hotel, the story remained the same as always: he was nineteen and worked in welding. He gave his dad's credit card details and promised to pay up at the end of his stay.

The stay ended early. A local police officer passing by recognised the truck's registration as one that was stolen. He went into the hotel and found it to be linked to David.

David Headley was arrested and transported back north.

Petrol had been present in David's veins from a young age. As a youngster he would go to car showrooms with his dad and collect the brochures. He'd study and read them so methodically that people would say he was going to be a car salesman.

Stealing cars was never just an act of simple vandalism or petty theft to David. While it was true he would often just take what was easiest, there was a love for driving and a love for cars that made such thefts desirable. Cars brought freedom, but there was also the giddy boyish thrill of the sound of an engine starting, the desire to go faster, the feel of pulling a powerful car round a bend in a country road before accelerating off to the next one.

The first car he bought was an Austin 1275 GT that cost him just twenty pounds. He got it when he was fifteen from a friend who lived on a farm. It wasn't road worthy in the slightest - the tires were bald, it wasn't road taxed, he had no insurance and it only had one working headlight. He drove it 5000 miles in total, often without paying for petrol.

As time wore on in Aberdeen, the car dealership he first stole from became something of a frequent target. In the space of three years he took a Renault 9, a Ford Escort, two transit vans and a Ford Sierra all from the same place. To start with it was easy because they didn't have a burglar alarm fitted on the building, but as David continued to steal from there they eventually added one to their security measures. But that didn't deter him as effectively as they'd hoped. Instead it fired up the competitive, adventurous side in David. He saw the alarm quite simply as a new challenge. To overcome the alarm all he had to do was be a better actor.

David knew that people only became suspicious when his demeanour or actions gave him away. The alarm meant he had to act cooler. He reasoned that if the alarm was set off and someone walked past to see him running around in a panic inside then they would have reason to suspect foul play. If, however, he kept cool and calm and just walked around unflustered inside then passers-by would assume him to be a member of staff and not think anything off it.

David was very good at playing it cool. He would even go so far as to apologise to neighbours and members of the public for the noise and inconvenience. His skills of deception were strong, and he was so good that he began pulling of feats of absolute audacity.

One day when he was fourteen he went by the showroom during opening hours and found keys left in the ignition of a gold Sierra 1600 GL. He took them and left the showroom planning to return later that night to get the car.

He returned not long after it closed and the staff had left. The keys going missing had been noticed and a transit van had been parked across in front of the car to stop it being taken out. David got into the car anyway and turned the keys in the ignition. Nothing happened.

The car wouldn't start. But David wasn't beaten, he had just been given a new challenge to take on, and so opted to put his acting skills to the test.

He phoned the AA. All he knew at the time was that the car wouldn't start, but upon explaining the situation to the AA he was informed that the rotor arm had been removed from the car and that is why it wouldn't start. David made out like the car was his and the cap had been stolen, in reality the store workers had taken it out to stop David stealing it. The showroom had another Sierra in it at the time, and it caught David's eye whilst on the phone to the AA.

"Would a rotor arm from another Sierra be able to fix it?" he asked.

"Yes, it would but I don't know where you'll get one in Aberdeen at this time in the evening," he responded.

"I do," said David. "I'll be able to get a hold of one no problem."

"That's great," the AA man said. He was impressed at David's ability to find such an obscure part at that time of day. David fobbed it off, almost flippant in his expression... "Contacts mate. Contacts."

He took the part from the other Sierra and fitted it in his car. He then put all of his weight on the backdoor handle of the Transit van and broke the door open so he could get in and take the hand brake off. After that it was easy for David to roll the van out of the way so he could reverse the car out of the showroom and hit the road.

This time round he got out of Aberdeenshire with ease. He kept pressing on from there, heading south. Soon he left Scotland six or seven hours later he was in London.

The wonderful thing about stealing from a car dealership that operated only daytime office hours was that vehicles were not registered as stolen until 9am the following morning when the staff came in for work. If David got in and took the car at 6:30pm the evening before, he would have a hefty head start on the authorities. Before they even knew to look for him he would be in an entirely different area of the country.

It took three days on this occasion for the police to catch up to him. He was stopped for taking too long to pull off at some traffic lights in London. The police suspected him to be a drunk driver, so he was made to take a breathalyser test.

He was clean. The police still pressed and interrogated though.

"Whose car is this?" they asked.

"It's a rental car," David replied.

"What hotel are you staying at?"

"The Royal Arms Hotel."

David was cool. He was together. He didn't falter, but one of the officers was suspicious. Eventually they allowed him to drive off.

In the car as he pulled away, David lapped up the rush of another great performance - another successfully avoided brush with trouble.

Thirty seconds later the police came racing after him. They'd clocked his car as one registered stolen when they had returned to their vehicle. David was arrested.

Grampian Police paid to have him flown back to Aberdeen on this occasion. David was hardly heart-broken, given that he now also got to go on a plane. He was escorted on the flight north by a single officer.

Upon getting to the plane, they found that they'd been booked in as a passenger and a stretcher instead of having the two seats that they actually needed. David wasn't in a stretcher, so in order to be accommodated on the flight the airline had to seat David and the escort in different areas of the plane. To David that made an already enjoyable experience all the richer, while the officer just had trial upon trial added to his job.

The flight was then delayed. The pilot came over the loud-speaker to announce that by way of apology for the delay ever passenger was allowed a free drink. David ordered whiskey, much to the dismay of the officer. He wasn't allowed to have it and the officer kept him hand-cuffed for the whole journey north.

When the wheels hit the tarmac in Aberdeen, a welcoming party from Grampian Police were waiting for David. They ushered him from the plane, through the terminal and out into a car for the hour or so drive to Inverness. Apart from the plane ride, it has just the usual drill as far as David was concerned. It wasn't the first time he'd been returned home by the police from various spots in the country. In Inverness it would be the same as ever - a visit to the Police station and then they'd deliver him home.

The way home from the Police station was different from usual. For a start, the police car he was in was unmarked. That didn't usually happen. The route they were taking was entirely unfamiliar. Something wasn't right.

CHAPTER 4

Looking out the car windows, David watched as semi-rural settings he'd never seen before passed by outside. His mind raced with questions: where was he being taken, what was going on?

"You've really done it now," came the one of the officer's voices from the front. A knot bound up David's stomach. He was actually scared of what might happen this time. This was all new, all unexpected. He had no idea what was waiting for him at the other end.

He was being sent to an Assessment Centre called Ferintosh House. The officers told him as they drew nearer to their destination and it sent David's mind racing again. 'What do they do at an assessment centre?' It sounded a bit sinister.

They arrived to see crowds of Police officers bustling around the building. "Is this place run by coppers?" David asked as he was collected by assessment centre staff and led through the building to a registration room. They didn't, it transpired. It so happened on the day of David's arrival that one of the care workers there had been arrested for having an affair with a 15-year old girl.

Inside the room waiting for him was his dad, David senior, waiting with clothes for his son. He was upset, and could only hold a gaze on his son for a matter of seconds before looking away in despair. Tears filled his eyes and his face went red and he fought to hold back the tears. He descended into sobs, occasionally glancing back at David jr. The young boy showed no emotion though - he didn't cry, he didn't feel sorry he was making his Dad cry. He thought it strange and a bit extreme a reaction from his Dad. It was the first time he'd ever seen his father cry, or in fact respond with anything other than anger towards his adventures.

Once he was signed in and had received the clothes, a female member of staff came in and led David away for his induction. His dad stood up as he left the room, tears leaking down his cheeks as he gazed on, lost for any further response. His stare was vacant as David was led away.

During his induction, the lady from Ferintosh house spoke directly to David. She got to the heart and expressed her frustration with his numbness to the turmoil he was causing for those around them. David was almost entirely detached emotionally from the situation. She was furious with him and told him he should be ashamed for making his parents cry.

They did more than cry though: they stopped speaking to him. David was unfazed. His life had been so scattered and separate from that of his family until that point that it made no difference. Up until then he'd only been making rare appearances for meals when he was at home, and even then conversation was strained.

Ferintosh House had twelve children in it - eight boys and four girls. It was staffed 24-hours a day and escape was made even more difficult by the fact the doors, though not always locked, were all alarmed.

The kids there were wild. They were the ones that needed to be supervised all the time. They were the ones that didn't fit neatly with the standard schooling system. David was by no means an exception among them. His time there was short and he was soon moved onto foster care. Through it all he didn't flinch.

He didn't care for his foster family though. His foster father was a music teacher and it wasn't cool to stay with a teacher. In the house with David were two girls, one of whom became his girlfriend for a short stint.

During his stay with foster parents he managed to stay largely out of trouble. It wasn't that he had calmed down particularly it was simply that he hadn't been there long enough to cause any real bother. In David's eyes though, it was his foster parents that were up to no good. He calculated how much he thought they were spending on the children in their house against the amount they were receiving in support - £60 or £70 per week - and found they were spending far less than they were being given. To David, that meant the remainder of the money was rightfully his. So four weeks into his stay, he took £140 from the house and ran away to Glasgow - the big city, where he could disappear into obscurity.

He never returned to foster care.

Loaningdale Approved School is where David found himself at age thirteen. It was a place born out of the desire to get disruptive children out of mainstream schooling, but it ended up with an even bigger problem of putting all these disruptive children in the same place. What emerged was a swap shop for knowledge on how to break a Yale lock, techniques for shop-lifting and how to steal cars most easily.

Students at Loaningdale were all put to work doing chores in order to instil a sense of responsibility in them. David was cleaning the shower block with a friend one day and the pair started having a carry on throwing water at one another. It escalated to the point where David tossed a bucket of water at his friend. He missed and hit a member of staff instead. The man he soaked was furious. "You want play with water then, do you boys?" he shouted.

Moments later David and his friend found themselves carrying a fibreglass canoe each to a pond on the school grounds. It was winter, the ground was frozen and snow was falling.

They found the pond covered with a layer of ice, but before they could back out or turn back to the school the boys found themselves forced to break the ice and plunge the canoes into the water. Their punishment was to get the canoes to the other side of the water through the ice and snow, with no paddles. All they had to propel themselves forward was their hands.

As David pushed through, his hands swelled bright red. His fingers were rendered useless by the cold, unable to bend, as ice cut his knuckles. He got to the other side soaking wet and frozen, his hands bleeding and extremities feeling like they were scarcely still attached to his body.

Back in the school he stood in a cold shower to get warm. The water, though freezing, felt like it was boiling his skin. He shivered and folded his arms, every muscle in his body bound tight. He no longer liked playing with water. Playing with water was bad news.

On the whole, Loaningdale didn't work out. David was deemed too intelligent to be in an approved school and his education was suffering by him being there, so the state paid for him to go to Holt Boarding School - a fee paying, private school. Even the uniform there was expensive - around £1400. David's parents had to pay half, with the state picking up the difference.

There were far too many spoilt brats around for David's liking at Holt. He saw being there more as an exercise in seeing how spoilt children behave themselves. There was a hierarchy in the school's student body which was policed by extensive campaigns in bullying. David hated it and didn't get involved.

What was horrifying for him though was the fact this school maintained pupil discipline to a stricter and higher level than any approved school. Classes would run from half eight in the morning until lunch time, after lunch there was an afternoon lesson and then sport followed by two hours of homework. It was everything David hated - routine, school work, no space to breathe. David rebelled in whatever way he could. He would not be in bed by lights out, turn up late for things. He sought ways to exercise his freedom.

Stealing the headmaster's motorbike and taking it for a spin round the grounds was a step too far though. He was expelled after just seven weeks there.

He was moved onto Geilsland School shortly after his expulsion, a place that was run more like a naval ship than a school. David was sent to board there when he was around fifteen. The school sat in the north Ayrshire countryside near the small town of Beith. It was run by the Church of Scotland's Board of Social Responsibility and operated more as a place of labour than as a place of traditional education. Pupils had to work instead of going to school. Entire sections of the school were built by the students. David was a stone mason.

At Geilsland, the boys were put through their paces. The headmaster was a former navy man - a short, well-built gentleman in his mid-fifties by the name of Alex Munro. He was known around the school as Sandy, but he was hardly on such informal terms with any of the boys. His military background was reflected in his style of law enforcement in school. He made the pupils parade three times everyday and would punch those who didn't have their shoes to a sufficiently high shine. Despite having a reputation as a strict disciplinarian, he was also known to have a good heart behind his actions. He wanted the best for the boys and showed them tough love.

David was caught by Sandy standing with his hands in his pockets one week. He was due to be allowed home on leave that coming weekend, but when Sandy saw him standing in such a casual fashion he poured a bucket of mortar over David's head and cancelled the leave. This was a no nonsense environment where bad eggs would learn consequences for their actions. Nothing went unpunished.

Boys will be boys though and despite being forced to conform there was fighting in Geilsland. The boys there could all hold their own which, for some, was exactly the reason they were there in the first place. These were the boys that had short fuses and that rubbed each other the wrong way. They were no strangers to conflict. They knew what it was to break a nose and have theirs broken. Whether the boys were fighters or not before they entered the school, they certainly became like that when they were there. They had to.

David was caught fighting by the depute head-teacher. Remember, nothing here went unpunished. He'd had a bucket of mortar over the head for having his hands in his pockets and fighting was much worse. There was always a tension in those minutes before finding out what the punishment would be. If it was just the belt it would be simple - that could be prepared for. Boys could ready themselves to face the pain, and they'd know it would be over quickly. But at Geilsland punishments could be more creative - there was anticipation.

For fighting, the depute head Ian Stanger lined up seven of the toughest, meanest fighters in the school and forced David to fight each of them in turn. Stanger - himself a big man, built for rugby or boxing - instructed that David would have a three minute bout in the boxing ring with each, one after the other.

The seven came in various shapes and sizes. Some were small and quick, others were bigger and slower but with jaw shattering right-hooks. David knew tactics had to spot on to emerge in any sort of reasonable condition.

They all lined the edge of the ring waiting their turn to try and give David a beating, and he knew psychology would play a big part. The trick was to appear better than he was in every facet of his skill as a fighter. To the big guys he would make himself seem ultra aggressive by getting in close to maul the smaller guys. To the smaller guys, he had to appear quick, so he would dance around the bigger slower guys avoiding their swings and nipping in to pop them in face whenever the opportunity presented itself.

In the end David fared quite well. But for a few bruises and knocks around the head he survived and held his own, even with the bigger opponents. He was a good fighter, better than the teacher had given him credit for. He'd done so well in fact that the depute head concluded that the belt would have been a more fitting punishment for David after all, but he couldn't punish him twice for the same offense. It was something of a small victory for David.

Regardless of what little victories were picked up throughout the day by boys in the school, they all still came to the eventual conclusion that it was best to conform, for the most part at least. The law enforcement was so strict and the punishments were so potentially unpredictable that it was safer to fall into line. For David, it was an experience unlike any other he'd had. School work meant being hands on, no one was amused by his antics and the people in charge actually knew what to do with him when he misbehaved. The escape from normality that he'd sought through crime and misdemeanours was in a strange way gained in the school. He settled down a bit, and seemed at last to be making progress back towards the tracks. His progress wasn't academic, but it was social.

The formality of Gielsland irked him though. He didn't like being marched to church every Sunday in a suit - as all of the boys were. He didn't like being forced to sit through the service and listen. It made him restless, but over time he learned just to get on with it.

Often the boys would be called in to carry out community projects, such as cleaning and building buildings. They eventually built a chapel on the school grounds - all of the labour was carried out by the boys using the skills they learned at school. David worked on a toilet block which extended the gym hall.

They were also encouraged in their artistic and expressive endeavours and each year the school would put on a pantomime. They performed 'Mother Goose' one year. Fortunately for David he was spared, being over-looked for a role amid the school role of 150 boys.

He left the school after one year, bringing his school career to a close with contact with his family having been restored. He was fifteen years old and headed out into the world with no qualifications, but nominated by the school as being someone "who will never be in trouble again." They presented him with an award to that strength as he left: 'David Headley - one that will never again get into trouble.'

After leaving Geilsland things seemed to be back on track in David's life. He went to college in Inverness for six months to study retail distribution, bought a Yamaha RD 50 motorbike for his sixteenth birthday and later moved to Aberdeen to get a job.

It was just the done-thing after finishing school for a young man to get a job. He worked as a trainee salesman for the same welding company his Dad did. That took him through the week meanwhile he stayed in a caravan on a campsite just outside Aberdeen. At the weekends he would head to Inverness for a second job as a check-out operator in a supermarket.

Although he loved living in the caravan and the personal space it afforded him, Aberdeen was a lonely place. He knew no one in the city and would spend evening after evening by himself initially. Before long he bought a Citizens Band radio to get himself connected and make some friends. Everyone had a channel and people could tune in and talk to one another to build friendships and relationships. It was a radio chat forum. Through it David made some friends, but it wasn't enough to settle him. He was bored.

All through his life he had never felt he was in the right place. Growing up in Inverness with an English sounding accent given to him by his English parents, he always felt out of place. Being in school and being a head taller than most made him feel out of place. Now he was in Aberdeen and the same thing was happening again.

What David felt was a gap in his soul. He felt there was more to life and he'd lived his childhood filling that with thefts and crimes of all sorts. Now he was in the real world working and hadn't committed any crimes for a year. But he still felt there was more to life. There were thrills to be had that being a trainee salesman did not provide.

A year after starting the job he returned to crime.

Although he left the job, David didn't leave Aberdeen, but for some short stints in prison. The most lasting impression was left by a short sentence at Glenochil Young Detention Centre. He was sentenced for theft at Aberdeen Sheriff Court and sent straight there for shock treatment. That's what the detention centres were for - to give a short, sharp warning to offenders not to mess with the law.

Upon arrival there David was put in a 'dubb box' - a small cell no more than 4' by 3'. There was only enough space inside to stand up or sit down. Lying down was out of the question. When he was let out of the box, he was marched everywhere and the officers in charge would come nose to nose with him to shout instructions in his face. It was like a military prison where they crushed disobedience out of the boys. Civilized conversations didn't happen there very often, so it was a rare thing when one of the officers took David aside and tried to talk some sense into him. David yawned in his face.

He was 17-years old when he found himself in a probation hostel. He'd been sent there after serving a few months in prison for theft. It was a place of residential accommodation for where society saw fit to take a group of troublemakers and stick them all together in the same place. It was little wonder many of them went onto re-offend. There were only six or eight of them in there at the time, a mixture of guys and girls. They got on but weren't all that close.

During his stay there David would take day trips out from the hostel to go and commit more crimes. In was on one such trip that he stole the first four door Vauxhall Astra GTE in Scotland. He took it from a garage in Aberdeen that he'd targeted many times before, a place he'd even been round the night to stake out the night before, trying to break the padlock of their gate with a crowbar.

The car was only just off the back of the truck when he took it, having been deposited in the showroom car park just 30 minutes previously. It sat in a lot of around a hundred cars, but stood out to David. It was new, it was powerful and a tasty piece of machinery. It appealed to David's every sense - the aesthetics, the new car smell, the sound of the engine. The power. The thrill.

He wandered around the lot, perusing the other cars just like all the other customers. Sunlight glinted off the bonnets of the vehicles lying all around. Because of his track record, David knew where to find the keys to the car: under the sun visors, the same as always. He got behind the wheel of the car, but because he was so sure of himself in doing the deed no one so much as thought to challenge him. Simple psychology in action again - he looked like he was supposed to be there. It was so much in people's faces that he was assumed to be a member of staff. Driving off was easy and no one gave chase.

The fuel ran out quickly. Just a few miles down the road he had to pull into a service station to fill up. That was the problem with new cars: they were delivered with barely any fuel in the tank. He filled up and drove off without paying.

It wasn't until arriving in Inverness that he realised the car had no number plates. The car needed them if was to hold onto it without giving away the fact that it was stolen. Waiting until it was dark, he pulled into a supermarket car park on the edge of Inverness and went hunting for an Astra with a screwdriver in hand. Before long he found one, unscrewed the number plates and fitted them onto his car.

These three thefts in quick succession (of the car, the number plates and the fuel) were nothing to David's conscience. In the three days prior to taking the Astra, he had been on a crime spree throughout the Scottish highlands where he committed just shy of fifty offences.

Sitting in a queue of traffic a couple of days later the game was up. The car had been undetected for a number of days, but some police officers had noted the stolen number plates that were fitted on it as David sat at a red light on Kenneth Street in Inverness, a street lined with shops and houses.

Through the passenger window, David noticed a car going past in the opposite direction stop suddenly. A man jumped out of the car and started sprinting over towards David. Plain clothes police. He had to move to avoid being caught, but the road was just one lane in each direction. The officer ran round the car to the driver's side, but as he did so David saw a gap and slammed his foot on the accelerator. The officer's arm came in through the driver's window just as the car pulled off, grabbing at the steering wheel. He caught it.

Adrenaline surged through David's veins and he grabbed tightly to the steering wheel with both hands, attempting to wrestle it free from the policeman's grasp. He pulled into the on-coming lane to get round the queue of traffic which remained at a stand still in front of him.

The officer held onto the car, dangling off the side as it sped up the street.

Fifty feet along the officer lost his grip and tumbled onto the road surface. His partner trailing behind radioed for back-up and issued an 'officer injured' call.

David watched the officer hit the road in the rear-view mirror then looked back to the packed road ahead of him. He swerved and weaved the car into space as far as possible. His mind was in a frenzy of panic and excitement. He searched for ways out of the jam. He was boxed in and couldn't move.

Moments later police cars appeared all around him. There must have been twenty of them, including ones with police dogs. Every available officer in Inverness surrounded David. His break-away was halted.

Officers surrounded the car and closed in on foot shouting. "Stay in the car, don't move." David turned off the car and did as instructed.

An officer reached in, pulled the keys from the ignition and handcuffed David to the door.

Inverness Police station was the destination, a place he'd been many times before for running away, thefts and fraud at hotels. David sat in a cell awaiting what was to come. An officer came to check on him, and said: "You might go down for murder because he's in a bad way."

A seed of doubt was planted in David's mind. The fall hadn't been that bad, he thought. Surely this was all out of proportion. Hopefully it was all out of proportion.

From sitting in his holding cell, he was taken upstairs to an office where he was met by a Detective Chief Constable. It was strange that he would be visited by an officer of such high rank. Something was amiss. Maybe the fall had been worse than he thought.

The detective stood opposite David and looked at him. His stare was severe, full of distain. He raised his hand and smacked David across the face. It was a firm hit. David didn't flinch, but raised his stare to meet the detective's. "Sit down," the detective snapped.

He began recounting what had happened, ending with the officer that grabbed the steering wheel falling onto the road.

Every question the detective asked was met with the same response: "I have the right to remain silent and I'm choosing to do so." Those words only made the tension and hatred grow in the room.

The session ended with a piercing final word. "If that officer dies then you're going down for murder," the detective said, the conviction in his voice making every word seem to hammer David between the eyes. If he dies? Murder? He looked back at the officer and tried to work out if he was being serious or if he was just trying to wind him up. But the officer's stare remained fixed. Massive tension had grown in the room and David was getting nervous.

Death.

Murder.

This was bigger than anything he'd ever done before.

The case was remanded from court for 110 days which David spent in Porterfield Prison in Inverness. It was a boring and lonely existence, spending 23 hours a day in his cell. He divided his time there between sleeping, sporadic reading and re-running crimes of the past in his head to try and work out how to do them again without being caught. Time passed slowly until he was brought to trial.

This was the first time in David's life that he had had a jury trial. For the most part he chose to sit in silence through the proceedings. He knew that keeping his mouth closed as much as possible would be the best thing for him. It was just him on his own after all, no family had come along - his own brother only found out about the trial when a friend at university showed him the story in the newspaper.

When he had been arrested the police took his clothes from him for use as forensic evidence. For the court case they had given him other clothes to wear, but they were so ill fitting David felt they made him look like a thug. Despite this though David felt things were going well.

He was called to the witness box for questioning. Under cross examination from the Procurator Fiscal he was largely keeping his cool, but the probing just went on.

"Why did you drive off when the officer approached your car?" he was asked.

"If someone came running across to your car and reached in the window, what would you do?" David responded, keeping a civil tongue. Being assured and cool was the key to projecting innocence.

Still the fiscal pressed: "May I put it to you that you knew at the time that the man approaching your car was in fact a plain clothed police officer?"

"May I put it to you that I f***ing didn't?" David snapped back. In a flash he felt all the innocence he was trying to project evaporate from the eyes of the jury.

David was found guilty not of murder, but of attempted murder. The officer that fell from the car had only suffered minor injuries.

After being referred to Edinburgh High Court, David was sentenced to four and a half years in prison. The sentence shocked him, but also brought new status. He'd been in prison so much over the past year that he knew he's have more credibility as a long term prisoner than he had had on short sentences.

He was taken from court and loaded into the back of a police van to be taken to prison. It was the start of a long period behind bars, but a period that would change him forever.

CHAPTER 5

Anger consumed David. It was irrational, but the switch had been flicked. At 20-years old he man found himself in prison for attempted murder. And now pacing his cell in Glenochil Young Offenders Institution, a mere 9' by 4', a frenzied desire for blood ate him up.

All it had taken was a throw away comment from an unknown inmate. Who was he? That didn't matter. What had he said? That didn't matter either.

All that mattered was the blade. David had to get a blade. It was time to mess this guy up. It didn't even matter so much to get the right guy. Any man would do.

Only in his cloud of red mist did this make any sense. All that mattered to David Headley in that moment was making somebody suffer.

In that moment the cell seemed so small, the walls so constricting. Being caged added fuel to the fire. The blade. Blood. David's breathing was heavy and his fists sodden with sweat as they pulsed, his finger nails digging into his palms.

He knew he was about to do something stupid, but it didn't matter. He was overwhelmed with hate and recklessness.

In the midst of it all, he uttered "God, if you're real then do something!"

Suddenly, silence.

He had stopped pacing. He became very aware of his breathing. It was heavy, it was loud. His vision felt strained and he blinked. Slowly he looked up on the cell walls and all around him. His tensed muscles, eager for conflict relaxed and he felt the anger drain from his body entirely. He breathed it out with one last heavy breath and a strange peace fell upon him. A desperation to pray followed. This had never happened to David before.

He went to the end of his bed and fell to his knees. He didn't know exactly what he was doing, all he knew was he had to do it. It was there was a weight in the air pushing him down to the floor. He brought his elbows up and rested them on the mattress and clasped his hands together. Squeezing his eyes shut as tight as he could, his need for God and the aimlessness of his life so far became massively apparent to him. On his knees he didn't know what to do, but a song he learned at primary school ran on a loop in his head:

"Good new, good news,
Christ died for me,
Good news, good news,
I believe."

After a moment of silently staring at the wall, wondering what to say he opened his mouth to pray. "God I repent of my sins and I give my life to you," he said. "But you have to have a purpose for me."

Purpose. In that moment David realised and acknowledged that he needed to have a reason for his life. For some inexplicable reason he then found himself trusting God to give it to him. It seemed so irrational to do such a thing, but yet it was also the most rational thing in the world to do.

Immediately a wave of joy crashed on top of him. The blade and his plan for it disappeared from his mind and he was overcome with joy, the likes of which he'd never encountered before. It was a rush like no other, and it consumed him and made his heart race and skip. Energy flowed through his body, pulsing from his heart, along his limbs right to his finger tips. He sprang up from his knees back onto his feet. He began to pace again, though this time out of joy not anger.

His soul was in celebration long into the evening. That night David went to sleep on his narrow prison bed knowing for the first time that he had a role to play. He was in God's family and now his life had a purpose.

In the weeks that followed, David wept. He mourned for the wrong he had done in life, he celebrated the goodness that God had shown him and grabbed hold of the message of the gospel: that by repenting and turning from his sins, believing that Jesus is the son of God and that He died for the sins of the world he could be forgiven by God. It became so real to David and it broke his heart with gratitude just thinking about it.

Two weeks after becoming a Christian, David went to the prison chapel on Sunday morning for church service. He was on the hunt for a Bible. Many of the cells had Gideons Bibles in them, but David hadn't been so fortunate. He had to go and acquire one for himself.

Prison was a place where the actions of a man were controlled for the most part by the masses. The masses decided what was and wasn't acceptable. Going to church on Sunday morning was acceptable and many of the men went along, though for most it was because inmates could pass things - such as tobacco or notes - between themselves during the service. David was there for much more sincere purposes.

To go to the chapel sincerely as a Christian was not acceptable. To leave it with a Bible was even worse in the eyes of the masses. As David walked back to his cell with his Bible in hand he walked through a tunnel of distain. Inmates lining the halls ridiculed and jeered him: "There's no way you're one of those Bible-bashers!" "Parole seeker!"

David kept his eyes on where he was going and walked through the taunts back to his cell. Previously he would have defended himself by appearing as intimidating and tough as he could muster, but now he walked through their spitting insults knowing he couldn't retaliate and preach the name of Jesus - the one who preached a message of love and forgiveness from God - without making himself a hypocrite. So he kept his head down and walked on through.

Back in his cell he fell to his knees once more and prayed, with the flaming darts from his fellow inmates words still lodged in him. He felt heavy and knew he had just announced to his block he was longer moving with the pack. "Lord," he said. "I'm prepared to do this but you're going to have to look after me."

From then on he stayed there a lot of the time, not out of fear or intimidation but rather out of spiritual hunger. He would sit on his bed and read for hours every day, seeking to know all he could about this God he's put his faith in. His knowledge previously had only come from going to church as a child and singing songs in his primary school's 'Good News Club'. So he sat and endeavoured to deepen his knowledge, to the point of shunning the recreation hour - the only time in the day when he could leave his cell - in favour of reading his Bible. It was a simple decision for David since the recreation hall had just one TV for the whole cell block, the facilities were sparse and the company often not particularly salubrious. He chose what he desired most, to stay in his cell, read his Bible and gaze out of his cell window onto the Ochil hills and dream of walking on them.

The new found faith that David had and the sudden changes in him brought about suspicion from prison guards. Like the inmates that taunted him when he'd walked with his Bible, so the guards also thought he was just pretending to be a Christian in order to get out on parole.

A few weeks into his life as a Christian, the Prison Fellowship started in Glenochil. It was a small group where Christians in the prison could get together and support each other and talk about the Bible. For David it was great, as it allowed him time away from his cell to gain guidance in his faith from people more mature and longstanding in their faith.

The group was run by Eddie and Frankie Macguire, a married couple who lived in the nearby town of Dollar in Clackmannanshire. They both exuded joy and David, like many, was drawn to them. Eddie was a short man of medium build from near Glasgow with a sharp sense of humour and an infectious chuckle. Frankie, his wife, was a gentle woman who carried a caring, motherly air. They would come into the prison once a week and run the group, which was a laid-back affair with biscuits involved and other food better than the normal prison fair. It was because of the standard of the food that many came, but Eddie and Frankie welcomed them all the same.

For David the draw was Eddie and Frankie themselves. When he looked at them he saw people that didn't just talk about faith - they had faith in a very real way. Here was a couple that were complete unqualified to be in the prison having no social work qualifications or experience of being in prison themselves, giving up their time to come and spend time with criminals. Their faith was evident on the outside and David took to them immediately.

Word of the group spread only through the prisoners themselves, as Eddie and Frankie weren't allowed in the cell block. David quickly excelled himself and would tell people about it so they could come along. Inmates were free to attend the Prison Fellowship provided they had behaved in the week previously, if they hadn't they had to stay in their cells. The group - about ten in number - would sit in a circle and share stories of how God had moved in their lives, share their pains and troubles, pray and sing songs led by Eddie.

Lives were changed in the Prison Fellowship. They held an event in the prison one weekend a year or so after they started the group which ran across the Friday, Saturday and Sunday where around thirty prisoners gave their lives to God. It ended with a time of worship led by a visiting band that was so powerful that even the prison guards commented on the strangely peaceful and joyous atmosphere that fell on the room during it. There was joy and David felt as if he was singing in the presence of God Himself.

That night a riot broke out in Glenochil. The prisoners were already in their cells when it kicked off. Inmates just started going nuts for no apparent reason, smashing up their cells, hammering on their cell doors and covering themselves in their own faeces. Hostility and hate hung in the air as the prisoners showed their worst. David sat in his cell and read his Bible taking shelter in its pages while murderers, rapists, armed robbers and the nation's most disturbed and violent men lost the plot in the cells around him. It passed over in the night, but David awoke the next morning in no illusions that to make it through his sentence he would have to stick close to his God for protection.

Over time David became known as a Christian throughout the prison and at Christmas time he was invited by the prison's Church of Scotland minister to join a choir for a Christmas carol service, despite him lacking any semblance of vocal ability. One of the members of the choir was a sex offender. David had already been threatened by some of the other prisoners about talking with sex offenders - they were after all the most hated men in prison and frequently subject to beatings. Spending time with them was bad news and some inmates told David that if he persisted to talk with such people then they would treat him as if he was one of them. David felt he was led by God to be talking with the sex offenders though, so he didn't heed their warning. The threats never amounted to much though.

On the night of the carol concert the whole prison attended, and they all booed. The joyous songs about the birth of Jesus Christ were drowned out by 400 angry men who hated the fact a sex offender was allowed to perform.

Some of them told David afterwards "We weren't boo-ing you big man but you shouldn't be with the likes of him."

David learned a big lesson through the experience, but it wasn't the lesson his contemporaries had been aiming at. Instead he saw prisoners grading themselves, seeing their sin as less than that of a sex offender because all they had done was rob a house or beat someone to a pulp. But there was no grading system in God's eyes, David realised and to grade and judge people wasn't his job. More and more he was being pushed to gain his identity and protection from God and not from how he was perceived in the prison. It was a shedding of his traditional defences and that left him very exposed. He would pray "God, I'm relying on you," and trust that he would make it through unharmed.

No one ever laid a finger on David and his spirits were kept up by reading his Bible and books of testimonies about how God had moved in people's lives, books supplied by Eddie and Frankie. All the while they supported him through prison fellowship and he even wrote to them on occasion using the single piece of paper he was allowed per week. He loved everything about that fellowship, not least for the people and the break from his cell.

It didn't last though. David became an adult when he was inside, having served three years of his sentence, and had to be transferred to an adult prison. That meant a new fellowship away from Eddie and Frankie. Perth Prison was the last place that David wanted to be transferred to. He prayed and asked God not to send him there, mainly because their Prison Fellowship was of a more traditional hue. He ended up there anyway.

In Perth he continued to write to Eddie and Frankie. He felt almost adopted by them as parents in the faith and would get in touch to share his struggles. They loved getting his letters and felt great affection for David.

Where Glenochil had been a modern prison, Perth was far more basic. It was full of older tougher criminals, men with more experience and history under their belt than the young ones at Glenochil. When they rioted it was serious, and one night they took over.

David sat in his cell locked in his cell. Some of the ring leaders in the prison had sparked off the rest of the inmates and the prison guards had run off, sealing the inmates in behind them. The prison belonged to the ring leaders now, and David was essentially a hostage. Out in the halls he could hear shouts and banging as hell let loose. And then smoke appeared.

Smoke was a bad sign. Six months previously during another riot in Perth prison an inmate had burnt to death in his cell. David saw smoke creep into his cell and immediately felt his head balmy with cold sweat. Panic gripped him. He immediately started searching his conscience and started to pray, "God, is there anything you need me to deal with before I meet you?" The walls between the cells were thin, so if fire was next door it would soon consume right through.

The heat rose in the cell block. David sat awaiting his fate and the smoke grew thicker and thicker. It stung his eyes and throat, drawing tears and coughs. This was it. The end.

The cell wall came crashing down.

The wall was ripped down by firemen who arrived in the nick of time. David was thankful to be alive. That night the prisoners roamed free in the cell block - it was still theirs.

Some of them broke the bottom of the block's pay phone so inmates could make calls for free. David phoned Eddie and Frankie, another inmate phoned the papers to tell them what was going on. Until then the prison authorities had been unaware that inmates had rioted, were now in control of the prison and had taken the rest of the cell block hostage. The next morning control was reclaimed by the authorities in exchange for some tobacco. David laughed at that - all his life was worth was some tobacco!

After six months in Perth, David was transferred back to Glenochil after it was reclassified to be an adult prison. David was glad for the move. It meant a return to more pleasant surroundings, to where he felt at home in the fellowship.

He stayed there for the remainder of his sentence.

A few weeks before the end of his sentence David was let out for prison on parole leave - a period of three days when prisoners are let out to find work and accommodation for when they got released properly.

Until then David had been unable to get water baptized - an outward signal of his decision to be a Christian. Prison hadn't supplied a sufficient facility. It was top of David's priority list, high above getting a job and somewhere to stay.

Eddie and Frankie organised it for him at a local church in the small Clackmannanshire town of Tillicoultry. When the event came the place was packed to the rafters with people eager to be a part of David's big moment, his moment of public declaration that he was now a Christian. Among them were people from prison fellowships, friends and his parents. The room buzzed with excitement and anticipation. This was a marker in time of a man who had lived life thrill to thrill, leaving a trail of destruction in his wake for he now had direction. He had left his selfish wrecking ball lifestyle behind. The Bible said he was a "new creation" and for David it certainly felt like that. His parents saw a different son to the one they'd broken contact with and lost into prison.

As he stepped down into the pool at the front of the church hall, it became apparent that David was too tall to be baptized length ways in the pool. Local minister Bill McFarlane and Eddie, who were baptizing him, decided the best way was to immerse him diagonally. One of them went either side and placed their hands on his back and chest. David made a public declaration of his faith in Jesus and then held his breath as they lowered him quickly under the water then back up - representing the death of the old David and the birth of the new one. As he emerged back up from under the water the church erupted in cheers and applause. David pulled the drips of water from his eyes and looked around the room; so many friends were there, so many people that cared and loved for him. He smiled a broad smile and thanked God silently in his head.

When he returned to Glenochil after his baptism David was regarded as more strange than ever before. For a prisoner to go out on parole leave and not use alcohol, drugs or women was considered madness. But he didn't care. He'd made his commitment and, if nothing else, at least people now knew that he was serious.

Prison taught David that he couldn't be a Christian and remain passive. To be a Christian in prison was to stick out like a sore thumb. It made him defiant in his faith, and gave him a fearless trust in God. Prison, in many ways, was his training ground in faith.

He wasn't sad to leave prison though. Instead he was massively grateful to have the simple freedoms of being outside on God's green earth. He loved that he could now breathe fresh air and feel the wind in his face. He loved that he could now walk in a straight line for an extended period of time (inside the straight stretches were always disrupted by corners). He also got to walk on the Ochil hills, and felt a deep sense of liberty to see up close the hills he'd gazed upon from his cell window for years. To smell and touch them was sweet. Never before had he known and appreciated such peace.

David was released from prison on the 2nd of February 1988. From there he moved in with Eddie and Frankie. They owned a home in Dollar, not far from Glenochil. It was 7am when he pulled on his old clothes - at this point the only worldly possessions he had - and walked out through the security entrance. Eddie picked him up to drive him to his new home.

He wasn't the first to move in with them after serving a prison sentence since they would often take people in. For David it was an extra special gesture though. He had grown to consider Eddie and Frankie his spiritual parents, the ones that nurtured him and supported him as he grew in his faith. They felt the same way about David: he was their son in faith.

Prison had been the birthplace of a beautiful connection between them, and now sitting in their kitchen, David looked upon the couple and smiled with gratitude. He was nervous about the move though since Eddie and Frankie had three young children. Meeting them was going to be nerve-wracking. He kept on imagining what must be going though the kids' minds - 'Mummy and daddy are having a criminal to stay again'.

The three girls filtered into the kitchen in their school uniforms to get breakfast. Their parents had already spoken to them about David's arrival, so they knew to expect him and to make him feel welcome. Frankie introduced them.

"Girls," she said softly. "This is David. He's going to be staying with us for a while."

"Hi, girls," David chipped in, raising his hand slightly at his side, as if to wave.

The girls smiled slightly and waved back, murmuring greetings.

Frankie took over again and introduced them one by one.

"David, this is Judith," she said pointing to the smallest of the three. "She is seven, and the one in the middle her is Fiona who is eleven." She pointed to the second tallest of the lot, then continued gesturing at the tallest of the three, "Susan is the oldest - she's twelve."

David smiled gently and nodded in acknowledgement. The girls looked back at him, before Fiona turned her attention to more pressing matters. "Great," she said. "What's for breakfast?"

Once the girls were fed and packed off to school, Eddie and Frankie sat and gave more attention to David. They chatted, ran over the rules of the house and got started on the necessary paperwork - social work papers, registering at the local doctor's surgery and other odds and ends.

By the time the girls returned home from, things in the house were much more settled. The paperwork that needed done was completed and the girls had had a full day away to get used to the idea of David being a new long term resident in their house. It wasn't that big of a deal to them anyway since they were used to having former inmates come to stay. Ex-convicts in the house was as much as part of life for them as homework or doing the dishes. They ate dinner together - their first evening meal with David being part of the family.

As the evening progressed in front of the fireplace David played board games with his new family and he began to relax in his surroundings. By the time the girls' bedtime came the initial feelings of nervousness and awkwardness had disappeared for all concerned.

He sat and chatted with Eddie and Frankie for a couple of hours more. They talked about God, about life and about family. They laughed together, and David felt at home.

When David eventually rose from the couch to go to bed - sleeping in a spare bedroom, downstairs by the front door - both Eddie and Frankie showed him through to his room door. They said their good nights and Eddie shook David's hand; Frankie gave him a hug. The house was to be treated as his own they said. He was to feel right at home.

He went into his room and closed the door behind him. Kneeling down at the edge of his bed, he looked up to the ceiling and prayed prayers of thankfulness to God for taking care of him and that prison was now over. He was safe and warm, God had provided for his needs. David never feared a lack of provision. In his mind his earthly father had always been a good provider and he was a mere man, far beneath the capabilities of his father in heaven. If the testimony books he'd read in prison were anything to go by, he had nothing to worry about. God was faithful to look after the needs of those who followed Him, and being in Eddie and Frankie's house made that message sink even deeper in David's heart. He said 'Amen' and got up from the floor.

It had been a long and tiring day, but climbing into bed sleep didn't come easily. His mind kept re-running things - his freedom, the goodness of God in his life. All through prison he had waited for this day, he had had a date written on his cell door that he dreamed of and now it was finally here, he'd reached it and was free. But now the date was gone things were different. Now he was left with a question that left him staring wide eyed at the ceiling: "what do I do now?"

CHAPTER 6

In prison David read books that captivated him with images of what church life was like. He read a great many books in his cell, but the two that stood out among them all were Colin Urquhart's 'When the Spirit Comes' and Dennis and Rita Bennett's 'Nine O'Clock in the Morning'. The authors had painted pictures of glorious bands of brothers united in cause and belief, loving one another and valiantly striving to live life as Jesus depicted in the Bible; people committed to one another and to being successful in living out the Christian life together. Church would be glorious.

His first time in church after leaving prison shattered that illusion. When out on parole leave he had been invited to share his story to a congregation in the town of Dunblane in Stirlingshire. After recounting how unruly he had been as a child he moved on to tell of how things progressed in his late teens. "And then I went to prison," he said.

"Good!" came a call from a man in the congregation.

David was unfazed at the time and continued on with his testimony. He tended to carry a confidence whenever he was speaking about God. It was only after he sat down at the end of sharing that he had time to register what had happened.

Something inside him felt jarred by the notion of a 'Christian' heckling him whilst he spoke in church about how Jesus had changed his life. It all seemed a bit naughty.

His church experience continued much like that after his sentence was over. Everywhere he went it seemed church wasn't what he had expected it to be. It was a disappointment, it was a distress. What had happened to the church he'd read about? Instead of being the most encouraging place he could be, he instead found that church was potentially the most discouraging place to be for a Christian. David had thought that church was a place where people looked out for one another, but instead found it to be full of hurting people who were more insecure and had it less 'together' than people who didn't go to church. It didn't make any sense.

Prison Fellowship had been fun and relaxed. The men in there were incredibly real and thought nothing of telling everyone if they thought one of the songs they'd sung that day was rubbish, or if they were struggling with some deplorable thoughts. This was a group of guys that had no preconceived ideas of church for the most part because they'd never previously been to one. After being involved in that, David's church reality was such a let-down. The standard of relationships seemed to lack and people didn't seem to be all that interested in one another's lives. On top of that there was no out-reach and David saw that as completely inappropriate.

Eddie and Frankie would take him to church with them. They watched him go through this experience, they saw his frustration when they all came back from church together and he would talk to them about it in the evenings before heading through to bed. It was something they'd seen men go through before after becoming Christians in prison. Many would get discouraged and disillusioned causing them to turn away from the church altogether, while others would get into the church culture and melt into the surface relationships and church language. But David kicked against it. Yes, he found it hard to take but he was so fired up in his faith and of such solid conviction about who Jesus was and what He had done in his life that nothing would shake him. Instead he wanted to seek for something deeper and not settle for the status quo.

Just a few weeks after leaving prison he had Eddie and Frankie join him in visiting a different church. It was bigger and had a greater focus on actually going out and serving the community and telling people about Jesus. They actually seemed focussed on growing their church and helping more people come into relationships with God. After one service, David said to Eddie and Frankie "Why don't we come here?"

The move of churches didn't end his hankering for something more. Regardless of the fact this church ticked more of the boxes he expected than the previous one, it still lacked. People still weren't entirely real. There was still an itch.

In David's view, God had changed his life and he was eager to tell anyone who would listen all about it. He wanted the world to know all about Jesus Christ and His miracle birth, death on the cross and resurrection. Jesus was alive in David's life and it was life to be shared. When others around him lacked that same passion to tell the world about Him, it made David frustrated. He took it upon himself to find people to share the gospel with and would wander the streets of Dollar stopping people to talk. He even went into the offices of a local architect every time the man was there working just simply to talk to him about Jesus. He hungered for more.

****

David had been out of prison and staying with Eddie and Frankie for just three months when he saw it - the phrase that summed up his attitude and hungering in life: "To know God and to make Him known!" He saw the words printed on a flyer somebody gave him for an organisation called Youth With a Mission, or YWAM. The flyer was advertising a course they were running at their base in Scotland called a Discipleship Training School, or DTS for short. The next day Eddie gave him a book to read - 'Is that really you God?' by Loren Cunningham, the founder of YWAM. In the book it detailed more of what YWAM was all about, they're determination to know God closely and tell the world all about Him. David devoured it in a day. It was the first book he'd read since leaving prison. It lit up his heart and his mind with new ideas and a hunger to be part of an organisation and a movement such as this.

After finishing the book and re-reading the flyer he was set - doing a DTS was the only way forward. The only problem was it was Wednesday and the course started on that Saturday. Time was tight. Without any further consideration he filled out and sent off his application that day, hoping and praying that it would all come through. Time however seemed stacked against him.

The next day the phone rang. It was YWAM. They invited him to go through for an interview on Friday, which was the following day.

He was driven to the interview by Eddie the following day. The YWAM centre in Scotland, Overton House, was based south-east of Glasgow in Dumbarton. David had no idea what to expect as the car pulled into the sprawling grounds. It was a hint of the surreal to him to see such beautiful grounds. Progressing through woodland, past a rushing river anticipation built in him as they drove.

Eventually they arrived at the YWAM building itself - a castle. His jaw dropped.

The castle had a grand entrance way, with a carriage arch before the front door to shelter incoming guests from the rain back when a horse and cart were the transport of choice. Carved into the stone on the building's external wall were the words "Let everything that has breath praise the Lord". Excitement grew in David. Before arriving the idea of being trained as a missionary had been appealing. The thought now had grown to be training as a missionary and living in a castle!

In the castle they were greeted and taken for a quick tour. Students were accommodated in dorm rooms, each containing around eight people. David thought it strange to live in a room with so many others, but soon forgot about it as the tour progressed and the size and resource of the castle captured his imagination.

He was then led along a corridor back to the main entrance of the building and told to wait in a small waiting area next to the staff office. Sitting there with Eddie, David quietly absorbed what he'd just seen, expressing only short mumbles of admiration about the facility. In response, Eddie answered with similarly short mumbles. A few moments later he was called in for the interview with the school leader.

Peter Mann was a sharply dressed man in his late thirties. He'd been drafted in to run the school from a YWAM base in England. After shaking hands and exchanging pleasantries with David and Eddie, he took a seat behind his desk and ushered them to sit down opposite.

The interview was just twenty minutes old when he brought it to an end. "I believe it is right that you should come here," he said to David. "We will count God's approval on the decision by him providing for you."

And that was it. The men shook hands and David and Eddie left for home. It was a matter of great thrill and wonder for David. Here he was with quite literally five pence to his name with an acceptance to study a course at YWAM which cost £1050. The course was due to start the next day and that meant David had to find a way to multiply what little he had to pay for school fees.

That night he prayed and asked God to provide, pouring out his heart.

David was up early the next morning waiting for the postman. Like an excitable puppy he waited by the mail slot for the letters to drop in, fully expecting that God would have seen to it for a mystery cheque arrive that would pay his YWAM fees. The postman came and dropped letters in. David scrambled to pick them up and sift through the pile. Bill. Bill. Junk mail. Bill. Nothing for him. He searched the pile again.

Still nothing,

Dejected, he headed back to bed. He had prayed and asked God and simply couldn't understand why the money hadn't materialised.

He was only back in bed a few minutes when the doorbell rang. Still dejected he wandered through to answer it.

Opening the door, a woman stood in front of him. He recognised her having met her a couple of times at a friend's house.

"Good morning," he said, almost wanting to tack on "what do you want?" But he didn't.

"Good morning, David,' she replied. "I feel like the Lord has told me to give you £700."

Something dropped inside of David and his dejectedness melted away in an instant. "Well, you'd better come in then," he replied, ushering her in through the door into the living room.

After calling YWAM to tell them about the money, he was told that they would trust God for the rest of the funds and that he was to come and move into the dorms at Overton House that day.

The first evening there, the new YWAM classmates sat in a room to share a night of testimony. It was the first chance that they had all together to really get to know one another. The room was full of students from all over the world. Only three of the people in the room for testimony night were from British Isles, with the rest coming from the USA, New Zealand, Germany and various other places. The Brits were just the school leader Peter Mann, David and a girl from England.

The stories people shared varied massively with the common thread being that the people ended up putting their faith in Jesus. When the English girl stood up to share, she told the story of how before she became a Christian she felt like God was following her. Everywhere she turned, she said, it seemed like she was bumping into Christians and having powerful experiences with God. "The final straw came when I borrowed a rubber from my friend and it had a Bible verse on it," she told the group.

The room fell silent and all of a sudden everybody felt very awkward. The American's in the room especially seemed particularly shocked. What sort of weird place was this that they'd come to?

Peter Mann quickly clicked into what had happened and stood up to break the tension. "I should probably clarify this one," he said. " In the UK, a rubber is like an eraser - not a condom." The room erupted in laughter, none more so than David.

Over the coming months in YWAM anonymous envelopes containing money arrived in the mail for David which paid up the remainder of his YWAM fees. They were answers to prayer and grew his faith. All the while, his knowledge and understanding of the Bible were improving too as he spent his days reading, praying and being taught. Often he, like the others doing the DTS, would go for walks on the school's beautiful and expansive grounds to pray and spend time alone. Aside from the serious implications of this time, David also saw it as a time and a space to have a bit of fun. One day as one of his classmates sat on a tree-stump praying, he snuck up in the trees behind them and whispered "Go to Africa," before silently slipping away. Later that day he overheard the same person telling a friend how they had heard the audible voice of God during their prayer time outside and God had told them to go to Africa. David didn't think he's be taken seriously and so quickly intervened and owned up.

Teaching on the DTS was taught in themed weeks. There was angel week, where students would spend the week anonymously leaving gifts and encouraging words and scriptures for one another. But David was most impacted by Sin Week. It was a heavy time on the campus where everyone was praying and asking God to reveal areas of sin in their lives. Everybody wrote their sins down on a piece of paper and worked through them for the week. At the end of the week they burnt them in a bonfire on the Friday evening.

The following morning they had a visiting speaker come and talk about different dark spiritual influences on the lives of people and how they affect behaviour. Given David's past, it was little wonder when he was called out of the group to be prayed for. The speaker laid his hands on David's shoulders and began praying for God to free David of the old dark, ungodly spirits that had affected him would be completely gone from his life. In that moment it was as if something in David broke, and he just started laughing.

Four hours later he was still laughing. It had been quite literally non-stop, and now his sides and face were in pain as he rolled on the floor. Such joy bubbled inside him that a deep sadness that had been in David's heart from a long time left. It was sadness from childhood, born out of the weight and trials of life. But now it had been laughed out after prayer. The sadness was now gone and from that day forward a light-heartedness and joy grew in him, and began flooding out of his very being.

Getting off the YWAM campus was a time of great refreshment for all involved. Six weeks into the course they took a trip to Edinburgh to share the gospel with people on the streets. A matter of weeks after that they went to a Christian Conference to learn from the world's top teachers. The conference was called 'Mission 2000' and was attended by just 800 people. It still was billed with some of the top teachers and ministry leaders in the world. Singing and praising God with hundreds of other like-minded people was a huge encouragement. The noise of 800 people singing songs of praise and joy in unison made such a glorious noise that everyone's spirits and faith were sky high. David had never experienced anything like it before, but it was three of the speakers in particular whose words impacted him. The status of these three was huge at the time - the equivalent to the prime-minister or top footballer in the secular world. Their very lives and the messages they preached touched him in such a powerful way that they made him want to be just like them and do more in the service of God; to love more, have more compassion, tell more people about Jesus, simply to act more of out a Godly heart.

One after one these speakers words hit his heart. First was Floyd McClung, a man who joined the hippy trail with his wife before they had a family and preached the gospel to those on the trail with a great number of people coming to faith in Jesus Christ. After they started having kids, the family moved to Amsterdam's red light district, where they raised the kids in a flat above a pornography shop. Amid his sermon, he pointed at David in the midst of the crowd and said to him "God used to call men and women to the jungle but now he is calling them to the concrete jungle." The words resonated in his heart. Until that point, David had imaged God's purpose for his life was to go to Africa or some far flung corner of the globe - but the concrete jungle? Before he had time to really digest the statement his thoughts were stolen by the life of a great man of the faith.

George Verwer was the man who founded Operation Mobilisation - a massive missions sending organisation that sends and supports people all around the world to spread the story of Christ and bring people to find hope in their lives through faith in Jesus. As a child he had all but one of his school classmates going to church by the age of 14. This story made David stand up and take note. "To know God and to make Him known" - the man speaking before him had lives this and was continuing to do so. David wanted that. But again, his thoughts moved on quickly to the compassionate words and obedient spirit of Jackie Pullinger - a woman who felt such a strong call into world missions that she bought a ticket on a round the world cruise and headed out to find where she was supposed to be. On the cruise she simply prayed that God would tell her where to get off. When she got to Hong Kong she got off the boat and there started reaching out with the message of Jesus to China's downcast. What her efforts eventually grew into was the St Stephen's Society, an organisation that brings practical help and the message of hope by faith in Jesus Christ to the weak, homeless and needy in China. In a smaller meeting at the conference she prayed for David and told him, "David, you're going to have a fruitful ministry with the poor."

The conference left David with much food for thought. Their words sat in his thoughts and he dreamed of how they would work out in his life. Africa was still on his mind. He was eager to get overseas, having never left Britain before. Fortunately, part of the DTS course was a missions trip that went abroad. His first foreign trip was on the horizon.

David's class was sent to Glasgow instead. The foreign trip, for this year only, was cancelled. He was massively disappointed. The reason for it was that the Glasgow

Docklands had just been regenerated and were hosting the Glasgow Garden Festival. It was a trendy place to be and crowds of people were descending on the city to be a part of it, and that meant there would be lots of opportunities to tell people about Jesus.

The YWAM team were housed in a church called the World Mission Centre in Glasgow's exceedingly rough area of Govan. The minister of the church, Alex Gilles, had bought the church for £1 after praying for God to provide a building for his congregation. That was their base for the week, and where they would bed-down on the floor overnight. The men and women stayed in different rooms of the church to ensure a level of privacy.

One night during the outreach, the girls came running through into the men's area of the church complaining there someone was banging on the outside door which led into their room. They didn't have to ask twice for David to spring into action as their macho protector. All he could find to arm himself with against a possible intruder was a brush, but that was enough for him. He went outside and walked round the church to the door which led into the girls' room. There stood a scruffy looking man of medium build banging on the door.

"Can I help you, pal?" David asked.

"I want tae talk tae God," came the reply in a thick, slurred Glasgow accent.

David paused. "That seems like a good desire to me," he said.

"Are you taking the mick?" the man shouted back. Without waiting for a response he pulled a gun from inside his jacket pocket and held it in David's face.

David looked down the barrel of the pistol and then his vision re-adjusted onto the man's face. The strange thing was the fear he almost expected to feel at that moment just wasn't there. David was not scared instead he was calm and bold. "That's a strange thing to bring to a church," he said. "Often people bring Bibles."

Just then the man broke down into tears. Amid his sobs he told David he had been using the gun to rob businesses in order to fund his drug and alcohol habits. "This is a great day to give this all up for good," David said. "It would be a great opportunity to turn your life around right now if you give me the gun."

So he did. The man reached out and placed the gun in David's outstretched hand. No sooner had the gun touched his hand than David remembered - just six months previously he had finished a prison sentence which lasted more than two years. He was banned for life from possessing a firearm. In his head he called himself an idiot. He didn't dare take hold of the gun properly for fear of putting even more finger prints on it. 'Why didn't I take hold of it with a cloth?' he asked himself. Now David felt fear.

The man's sobbing continued. He said he could see God in David and that he wanted that too, before making a booze-fuelled repentance, grabbing the gun back and running off. As he did so David shouted after him "Get rid of that thing!" and prayed that the gun ended up in a drain that night, partially so the man would get out of crime and break his bad habits but also so a gun with David's prints on it wouldn't end up in Police hands.

He left YWAM after his six-month DTS was finished and headed to Edinburgh to take up a post with YWAM

Edinburgh. There he was assigned two tasks - to help run a church-based DTS course and also to do youth work for a church. There he would work under YWAM Edinburgh leader Jerry Bishop.

Within three months the work he'd been assigned to in Edinburgh had fallen apart. Jerry had been deep in prayer and came to David. "David, I've been seeking God and I feel like He has given me a word for you," he said. Excitement sprang up in David. This was it: the call to do missions in Africa.

"The word is this: those who used to steal should work."

David felt the wind immediately drop from his sails. He was deflated. Reality hurt.

In the days that followed he got himself a job i a cardboard box factory in the Gorgie area of Edinburgh. He worked it for a few weeks and then decided to head to his parent's house for Christmas.

His parent's had moved since David had gone to prison and now lived in Markfield, a town near Leicester in the heart of England. He hitchhiked to get there.

Standing at the roadside with his thumb out, a thought crossed his mind that he had never been given a lift by a Christian before. No sooner had the thought crossed his mind than a car pulled up to give him a lift. The man who was driving it was a Christian and was in fact a distant relative of Jackie Pullinger.

They chatted the whole way down and the man drove David to his parent's door. As David got out of the car the man leaned over the passenger's seat and handed David a piece of paper. "If you ever want to come to Poole our job-market is really good," he said. David looked at the piece of paper and then back at the man. "Give me a call," he said.

David did just that a few days after Christmas.

CHAPTER 7

David moved to Poole in Dorset just a few days after New Year where he lived with John and his wife. Within a week of being there he had a job working as the parts assistant for the local branch of a national car garage chain.

It was a job he excelled in and promotion came quickly. As much as he loved the work and getting to work with cars, he had to get over a sense of rejection he felt at now having to work hard in a normal secular job after the thrill of being a missionary in YWAM.

Life became comfortable in Poole though. He continued to stay with John and his wife, and had no ambition to move on, his income was healthier than ever, he was provided with meals and had his washing done by John's wife and he was able to buy a car - a black 1966 Ford Cortina, which people called the Batman car. But David's heart was in Edinburgh.

Just before he left to move to Poole, he had become friends with a girl. Since he'd been down south their relationship had grown and they were speaking on the phone for at least half an hour a day. On his days off David would drive up to Edinburgh to see her.

After nine months, he quit his job, moved back to Scotland and married her.

After marriage a family followed soon after. His wife bought a home on Ferry Road in the north of Edinburgh and David, with a real need to provide, got a job working for a burglar alarm company where he surveyed to check the suitability for properties to be fitted with alarms. It was a matter only of poor background checks in the security industry that allowed a former criminal who had been involved in house breaking to get such a job.

From there he moved on to be a touring caravan salesman. As a child he'd been told he would make a great car salesman, such was his love for cars and ability to communicate with people. With criminal convictions and motoring offenses now on his record, a caravan salesman was as close as he was going to get.

All the while he was involved in the Baptist church. It was there that he was approached and asked if he would mind driving a caravan through the centre of Edinburgh on a Friday night to be used as a soup kitchen. No one, despite their compassion and desire to show love to those on the streets of Edinburgh, was comfortable commanding the control of a caravan let alone on busy city streets. David on the other hand spent his days at work moving caravans all over the place and would reverse and put them anywhere.

The soup kitchen outreach led him out into the graveyards of Edinburgh city centre at night to find homeless people to feed and minister to. It was a great opportunity - throughout his time working in the secular world he'd had an interest in Christian ministry work, particularly work involving caring for the poor, the homeless, and those with addictions.

One night when he was out speaking to people and dishing out soup he prayed internally and told God he wanted to be effective in what he was doing. In response, God told him clearly that to be effective he was going to have to humble himself and show God's love to people.

As the night progressed David came across a man sitting under hot air vents round the back of Edinburgh University. In his hand was a can of Special Brew, he stank of urine and had days old vomit dried onto his clothes. The smell coming off the man made David feel physically sick. But God had spoken and he knew that he had to humble himself and show God's love. So he simply sat down on the ground right next to the man and started chatting away to him.

But such immediate responses were not always how God impacted David. Sitting in the caravan one night, he'd been chatting to one customer for a number of hours. The man he was chatting to was homeless and was asking if he could stay in the caravan that night. To allow him to do so was entirely impractical, seeing as the caravan was stored in a secure lot several miles away.

God put a burden on David to invite the man to stay in his home. But with a wife and kids at home he first decided he needed to check it was okay with his wife. With no mobile phones to call home, he quickly drove home and asked his wife if the man could stay. She said yes, so David jumped straight back in the car and drove straight back to find the man and issue the invite. But when he got back to the soup caravan the man was gone. He couldn't find him at all. Then God spoke to David: "how far will you trust me?"

As the soup kitchen outreach continued, it also grew. The caravan was upgraded and replaced by a former mobile bank, which was called 'The Care Van'.

The vision for the van had come from a Baptist minister who had a dream of a holistic approach to homelessness. People from over forty different churches and many different denominations were involved in the care van. It was often said that the volunteers got more from the project than the clients themselves. It was a great chance to deal with undesirable people and many found it very difficult. Judgmental attitudes came to the surface and people had to deal with their own heart issues towards the homeless.

Meanwhile at work David was making a decent living. He worked hard but had a reasonable level of success with it. He liked selling caravans, there were certainly worse jobs, he reasoned, even if it was a bit boring. He couldn't have known that things were about to get a whole lot more interesting.

One day at work his boss came to him as he sat in the office with a mug of coffee.

"David," he said. "I need you to patch up one of the show caravans."

"What for?" David replied.

"Just do it, will you. I want to sell it on at list price."

"You want to sell a show caravan as new?"

"Yeah, there's no problem there though it'll be as good as new. Go and get to work on it for me so we can flog it."

David paused for a brief second. This flew in the face of his faith; it flew in the face of simple honesty. "Well, I can't do that," he said. "I've got a bunch of holidays I've still to take so consider this my notice period."

Then he left. He went home to tell his wife what he had done. His decision didn't prove to be a popular one, and he was given a hard time about it from family friends, especially given that he had a wife and 18-month old son to provide for.

His prayer life was filled with a new urgency from that moment. Every morning and evening he would fall to his knees next to his bed and cry out to God for help with his finances and to get a job. During the day, he applied for jobs. On the off chance God didn't provide a job for him, he went to visit his bank manager to say that there was a chance the mortgage may not get paid that month.

Within days a job with Bethany Christian Trust, an organisation offered care to homeless people and addicts, came up. David applied and felt God speak to him and say "You will work for Bethany."

There was only one other applicant for the job. After a two rounds of interview the final round of the recruitment process was a home visit.

He didn't get the job.

David was down-hearted and got a job as a deputy manager in a supermarket, after being out of work for two weeks. He maybe didn't have the job he'd hoped for but at least he had a job. It was a well-paid one at that.

Six-months later he was approached by Bethany to apply for another job that had come up with them. He did and got it.

Bethany was turning an emergency hostel into a rehabilitation centre for drug and alcohol abusers. David was taken on as a project worker. At last he was where he wanted to be - in full-time Christian service.

In the days that followed his appointment, David was reflective. God had been true to His word - David was to work for Bethany. What he realised though was that he had added a bit to what God had said. David had himself added details of which post God would have him work for Bethany. By not getting the first job he'd applied for with the organisation, it was as if God was saying to him that yes, he would work for Bethany, but it would be the job God wanted him to have, not the job David assumed he was to have.

The prayerfulness of the staff was an inspiration for David, as they were constantly seeking God. They heard God's voice when they prayed. One of David's colleagues was a man called Sandy. He lived in Edinburgh's desirable Morningside area, owned properties and had lots of money. He came to David one day and told him that God said they were to have a 'David and Jonathan' type of relationship, by which he was referring to two characters in the Bible that had such a close friendship that it is said their souls were knit together.

One day they were having a conversation about money and David said "You have to have money to make money."

Without blinking, Sandy replied "Okay then, I'll loan you money so you can start making money."

The money he gave was used to buy used cars from auctions, which David would then repair and sell on. It was a way of adding a bit extra to his income.

Often the Bethany staff would hold prayer meetings that would start at 7pm and go right through to the small hours of the morning. God would move in those meetings, giving encouraging prophetic words for people and healing them.

One night Jill, the deputy manager at Bethany, said to David in one of the meetings 'God says you are like a hard-boiled egg, but He is going to reverse the process and make you soft-boiled." For David, that spelled a softening of his heart. It meant that deep down inside him God was doing a work to bring about real compassion and care that was previously beyond him.

The prayer meetings were full of desperation before God. Everyone on the staff knew that apart from God they had nothing to offer these men that were coming struggling with all manner of drug and alcohol addictions. David, like many others, would pray "God, if you don't move then what do we have to offer these men?"

The problems facing the men that came to rehab were real. They were issues and addictions that threatened their very lives and the staff felt a burden not just for the physical and mental health of the clients, but also for their spiritual health - they needed God's help to ensure not just that they got well and off the drugs, but also for the men to know God personally. There was even an instance where one of the clients died in rehab such was the destructive force of his addiction.

Personally David was forced to rely on God in a way that he never had done before. He led morning devotion times every day which was a one hour bible study. The burden of how important that time was for the clients made him seek the Lord all the more to make sure he had something really great and encouraging to say that was going to help the men. It was urgent. He needed a 'now' word that was going to change people's lives.

The job came with heavy strain. Shifts often lasted 24 hours making it physically very tiring, as well as emotionally, spiritually and mentally exhausting. But the long hours also had a negative effect on family life, which caused some strain. Full-time Christian service was certainly not for the faint of heart.

Part of David's vision going into the job had been to create a family atmosphere for the men that were in rehab. In order to make that happen he began taking his family with him to the rehab centre for Sunday lunch every week. It was met with the desired response. The men at the centre felt trusted, they felt included, they felt loved and restored that someone would still welcome them into the warmth of his family amid the trials of coming off an addiction.

The clients also came into their own on trips away when they would go with David on caravan holidays and visits to adventure parks. David thrived too when taking them outside to learn to function again in the outside world and that didn't go unnoticed.

Before long he was asked to head up a new project for Bethany which involved running a residential farm for the men where they would learn new skills in joinery, farming and car mechanics. The project excited David massively, not least because he would live onsite with his family and, of course, get to play with cars.

In the beginning the meetings for the project were thrilling and full of anticipation. David met with architects for three months planning and creating the ultimate care unit, which was designed to be like a big house. The idea was to make it feel homely.

Nine months after the meetings began the plug was pulled on the project due to funding issues. In that nine months David had done basically no ministry, and he hadn't been doing what he felt called to. Frustrated with the project's failure, he asked Bethany to make him redundant. They reluctantly obliged.

The work had been all consuming, however fruitful. David's faith and relationship with God had been pushed deeper, but the time was right to move on. His next job was also a ministry role, this time with the Church of Scotland.

Now he was working as a team leader at a homeless unit in Edinburgh's Cowgate. It was a very different ministry experience to the one he had just come out of at Bethany. For one thing, there was much less prayer. At Bethany there had been at least an hour of prayer everyday, but this new place was much less inclined that way. Instead their focus was on good social work practice, almost above all else. Whereas part of the job at Bethany had been about sharing the Gospel of Jesus Christ with people, evangelism was almost frowned upon in his new job. The very ethos of the place challenged David as a Christian. How could he work for a Christian organisation and yet find prayer and evangelism not only pushed down the priority list, but almost discouraged? The people that surrounded him on the staff had a church connection but had not given their lives over entirely to Jesus.

The environment was stifling to David in more than one way. It was a place of professional excellence that didn't stimulate David's real passions - for ministry and prayer. Sitting in an office labouring over case notes was a mental drain by comparison, though he could also see it was a good discipline for him. The pay was also substantially better than he had been used to, so the financial strain for his family had been eased.

While working for the Church of Scotland, David was continuing to attend a Baptist church and was now serving as a deacon on the board of deacons - a role which was essentially like being an elder. A friend of David's had told him about a meeting he had recently attended which was with a strange team of people from Toronto, Canada. At the time a massive faith revival was in full flow in Toronto, with people coming to faith in Jesus and experiencing the power of God in all manner of ways - healings, prophecies, fits of joyous laughter. These goings on had been met with two main responses, the first being that of sheer excitement where people just threw themselves into involvement with it and believed everything that was happening. Others were sceptical. David's friend fell into the latter category but had gone along to see for himself what was going on.

The meetings in Edinburgh were held in the Church of Scotland's Assembly Rooms on the city's George Street, a street lined by upmarket clothing shops and restaurants.

After going to the meeting, the man told David "I don't know what happened, all I know is that I feel like $1millon and closer to God - you should go!"

So he did. A couple of nights later David went along to see what was going on. The meeting he went to was called 'Catch the Fire'. There were literally hundreds of people there when he arrived. He had never seen anything like it before, especially not in Scotland on a Wednesday night! That night between 3000 - 4000 people gathered in three different venues across the city to be a part of the meetings.

The atmosphere buzzed with anticipation and excitement. People were genuinely expecting God to blow in through the doors and move in powerful ways. After a time of worship, the preacher shared a message about times of refreshing. "Loads of people all over the world have been giving, giving, giving and God is going to bring times of refreshing," he said. "Shortly we are going to have a time of prayer and we strongly encourage people to come up and receive what God has for them!"

David didn't need a second invitation. He was right up at the front of the hall to receive prayer. Within seconds of someone starting to pray with him, he fell to the ground. As he lay on the ground he felt a heaviness lift off him and a massive sense of joy begin to surge through him. His spirit suddenly felt very light. It was, as the preacher had said, a time of refreshing.

There were many more meetings like it afterwards and David was at many of them. He then became very curious and eager to explore what God was doing, so he started a house group to do just that. At the group they would have a time of worship, where they would sing songs of praise to God and then they would ask the Spirit of God to come and be with them. Their prayer was answered and the group began having encounters with God in the meetings.

Around the same time as the group started, the pastor at the Baptist church where David was a deacon left. The church was stale and the life was draining from it. Encouraged by his recent encounters with God in his home group, David began telling people at church about the wonderful things that were going on. His comments were not well received. David was, clearly, pulling in a different direction from the rest of the pack in some respects.

With the church having lost its pastor he wanted to show support. He decided to start attending an evening service at a new fellowship that was starting in Edinburgh fully immersed in what was happening in addition to attending his own Baptist church in the morning. In the morning he would be a responsible deacon and by night he would go and explore the wilder things of God. It was a problem free solution to the problem.

Or so he thought.

After the service was finished one Sunday, two of the other deacons approached David.

"David," one of the deacons said. "We don't feel that it is right for you to go to another church in the evenings.

"Why?" he asked.

"We feel that you have the ability to influence other people to do the same thing. If that were to happen it could cause the entire church to collapse."

Indignation rose up in David. He couldn't believe what he was hearing. "That's nonsense!" he said. "Surely you're not being serious?"

"We're being very serious," the other deacon chipped in. "You're flitting between churches could cause this church to collapse and die. So you're going to have to make a choice. Either you commit yourself just to this church or you leave."

That was it spelled out in no uncertain terms. It angered David that he was being put in such a position, but in essence that made his decision all the easier.

"Fine then," he said. "I'll leave."

After departing from the Baptist church, he and his family joined the church he'd been going to in the evenings - 'Sunrise Christian Fellowship.' It was a new church started by a group of New Zealanders. It was a place full of incredibly passionate people who cared deeply about reaching out to the city and telling people about Jesus. They preached and taught of God moving in supernatural ways and expected Him to hear their prayers and intervene in their lives and in the lives of others. The church's expansion was explosive. Many had tried and failed to plant churches in Edinburgh over the years, but Sunrise took off like a rocket. Within four months it went from having a mere handful of people in attendance to having a four hundred strong congregation. God was moving.

It didn't last long though. The church collapsed and fell apart as quickly as it had grown up because of issues in people's personal relationships. As far as church life went, it was back to the drawing board for David.

CHAPTER 8

David's love of driving was no secret to anyone. Other than Jesus, cars were what he predominantly talked about. While at Bethany he was asked to drive a truck to Croatia as part of a humanitarian aid project. It was a time of great unrest in Bosnia where an act of modern day genocide was taking place. It was the story dominating news headlines everyday with report after report of families running for their lives. It was a land being ripped apart. At the time of asking though, David was so consumed with work at Bethany that he had no idea of what was going on. He had never even heard of Croatia, nor had he so much as left Britain. So with a scarce knowledge of what he was getting into, he agreed to do it.

So the mission was set. He would drive a 7.5 ton truck full of food, clothes and medical supplies into the conflict zone. The truck he was driving was owned by a church in Fife. Horror gripped him when he saw it for the first time. It was bright orange with a rainbow painted on the side. It was the sort of vehicle that looked like it was owned by hippies, and just screamed for border guards and customs officials to take a special interest in it. The trip was planned to take seven days to get there and back, and David would be doing it with another man - one who had been hand-picked by the church.

David's driving companion was around fifteen years' older than him and a diver to trade. In supplying a truck of such stunning loudness, it became apparent within a short time from setting off that the church had also supplied a rather pedantic man to transport the aid. Instead of two Christian men travelling on a merry march as a band of brothers united and agreed on Christ, what actually transpired is that the travel companion was not a Christian at all, and would go to great lengths to disagree with David on every single possible point.

The truck had a big fuel tank on it, so the pair didn't have to stop for fuel until they reached Milton Keynes, near London. They stopped there and filled up the tank, got a snack and David took a short fleeting break from his companion to re-group. It seemed that fuel stops would be moments of great rest and refuge for the trip - a small window to take a break from the wheel, get something to eat of drink and a break from present company. They were given a fuel card for the trip to pay for everything, seeing as filling a tank of that size was a task of massive expense. So having filled up, refreshed and paid they jumped back in the cab and hit the road again.

They drove on to Dover where they boarded a ferry and sailed to Calais in France. As the truck rolled out of the ferry on the other side of the channel, David reached a life landmark - his first time on foreign soil. His previous record distance of trip had been to the Channel Islands. There was no time for long breaks or to stop and sleep on this trip. It was constant, with stops made only for fuel. They had made good headway into France before they had to stop again.

Having filled the tank, David went inside to pay. The filling station attendant rang the sale through the till and David went to his wallet to get the fuel card. As he flipped his wallet open though, the fuel card wasn't there. He frantically patted his pockets to see if maybe it was in there. No luck. So he searched his wallet again, glancing awkwardly at the man behind the till so apologise. It wasn't there. He had left the fuel card in England.

"I'm sorry, I seem to have lost my fuel card," he said the attendant sheepishly.

"Pardon, Monsieur?"

"I said, 'I seem. To. Have. Lost. My. Fuel. Card. I have no money to pay." David said, making exaggerated gestures with his hands in a bit to explain himself, as if by waving his hands enough the man behind the till might suddenly speaking English.

"Argent? Vous devez payer."

David had no idea what the Frenchman was saying, so tried for a solution. "Do you speak any English?"

"No."

Both men looked at each other in frustration. The man at the till wanted paid, David wanted to pay but couldn't. Between them they were achieving nothing.

An hour and a half later, following a procession of managers and phone calls the fuel was paid for and they left. The credit card company had faxed through the details which would allow them to pay for items without actually having the card with them. It didn't help much though as the same procession of staff and multi-lingual misunderstandings followed every time they stopped to refuel. The whole debacle informed David's first opinions on a number of European nations as they went. Namely, the French felt they were superior and made little effort to communicate with them and the Germans could speak English but chose not to.

As the truck rumbled on into Austria, the one thing the pair were thankful for as they drove was the minimal trouble they had had at borders. Having travelled from the UK into the France, and then on through Belgium, Germany and now Austria everything had been very straight forward. Things were going to plan, apart from being searched occasionally for being in a hippy truck.

Things changed at the Austria's border with Slovenia. Officially the border closed at 9pm, but arriving there at 7pm they were told by the border guards they would not be getting through. It seemed ridiculous that such an assertion would be made by the border guards with two hours left until closing time and no reason given for their stance. There was no question in David's mind or that of his travelling companion that the guards were after a bribe.

But there was a problem as they considered what to do. Before they had set off from Edinburgh, the church that had supplied the truck had told the pair very specifically not to give bribes since they were working for Christ. The church had proudly told the story of a minister who had gone on an aid mission just like theirs and chose to sit in a holding area for three and a half days because he refused to pay a bribe of around £20. David disagreed with such a course of action. As far as he could see, bribes were a cultural acceptance and the minister in that story had made himself unavailable to his church for three and a half days, was late with the aid and had wasted three days over the matter of £20. Who won here? No one.

The Slovenian border guards got their money and the pair progressed. Time was an issue here and it was worth paying a small fee to get the aid there on time. It didn't even matter that his driving partner disagreed.

They passed into Slovenia through a tunnel. Not only was David now abroad for the first time, he was also now in a former communist state for the first time. He had expected to feel different being beyond the Iron Curtain - as if the very air and atmosphere of the place would feel strange and cold. In reality he found the people to be friendlier than they had been in Austria.

The Slovenian border with Croatia was the next major hurdle. After driving through no man's land to get there, they arrived to the most awkward border staff they had encountered on the whole trip. The level of bureaucracy made their heads spin, with hurdle after hurdle presented to them by the border officials. They were in for a long wait to get into Croatia with the aid.

During the wait David got talking to another man who had been forced in a long wait. He was an English soldier that worked for NATO and drove a truck back and forth over the border every week making trips to England for aid and resources and then returning with them. He was no stranger to the border officials. They knew him and knew what he was carrying and yet still insisted on searching his truck every time he crossed, making him repeatedly fill out the same forms and then making him wait. Typically, he told David, the border guards made a trip that should have lasted seven days last thirteen or fourteen days, simply because the border guards didn't think they should be there and wanted to give them a hard time.

David spent 17 1/2 hours at the border before being allowed through.

Once in Croatia they were met by a guide, who led them along pot-hole ridden, winding country roads made more for Ladas than they were for trucks. All along the roadside were shells of cars which had broken down. In eastern European culture, it seemed when something broke people would just take the parts of the car that were of use to them and abandon the car. The thought of actually fixing the car was not one that even seemed to be considered.

The guide took them to a hotel where they would stay that night, a place set in rolling green hills with a river running by the side of the building. It was the first time they had had proper beds to sleep in since leaving Edinburgh. The hotel complex where they were staying had been built just prior to the war starting, and they were the first tourists to stay in it. It was completely untouched by the war and everything in it was brand new and immaculate. It seemed the war didn't reach all areas of the country.

The next morning they went for breakfast in the dining room. The room was set out to seat around 300 people, but was occupied only by David and his driving partner in one corner and a small hunting party in the other. The meal set before them was a feast. There were thirteen different sorts of meat on platters, a pig roasting on a spit with an apple in its mouth and various other side dishes. The pair of them ate in near silence, enjoying the food and watching the hunting party in the far corner who were, by contrast, were very loud. They would take it in turns to stand up and speak as they ate. The speaker's voice was get higher in volume and pitch and he got caught up in whatever he was saying, then everyone else around the table would jump to their feet and start shouting. Neither David nor his partner had any idea what was being said. It sounded like the hunters were angry, but they were actually quite peaceable.

The refugees lived in a different world. It was later that day that they got to them. Amid rubble and streets vandalised in the conflict, people were struggling to get by. They met people who had lost parents, brothers, sisters, children, friends and neighbours - people who had seen their own loved ones shot dead before them. These were people very much affected by the war, whose lives depended on the hand me downs and charity. The refugees were given £2 per week by the government to live on. Of that £2, most would spend around half of it on plums, which were then used to make a strong alcohol, and coffee. Both were so they had something to give people who visited their homes. Even amid slaughter and strife, living on the bare minimum, the locals still spent half their weekly budget on hospitality.

In a coffee shop David met a solider that was off on two days rest. The soldier told him how he was friends with the people he was fighting against and had actually gone to school with many of them. It was just a matter of how their hand was dealt that the friends had ended up on opposing sides. David asked him how he coped with fighting and having to try and kill his own friends. The soldier told him that they all agreed that in the day time they would just shoot at trees to give the illusion they were fighting one another so as to appease their generals. By night they would all meet up and play cards together. It only worked until the generals worked out what they were doing and moved them on to fight in a different area.

Not long after returning from the trip David left to work for the Church of Scotland. The trip had change him in his attitude towards his work. Having met people that were facing real hardship caused through no fault of their own, it affected and started to slightly harden his attitude towards drug addicts and alcoholics at home in Scotland. Somehow their struggle now won less compassion from him than it had before. It wasn't that he didn't care anymore it's just that they often didn't seem to really want help. He was left increasingly eager to go on more humanitarian aid trips, to bring the love of God in a real practical way to people that really needed it.

Christmas passed that year and David was on-shift at the hostel on Boxing Day. It was quiet at work with not much doing and he was sitting reading the Edinburgh Evening News. In the headlines were stories of war in Kosovo and Albania, and then a story about an Edinburgh-based charity called Edinburgh Direct Aid who had touring caravans they wanted to take to the conflict zone to set up a refugee camp. All they now needed were people and 4x4s to get them there. Reading the article David felt his heart quicken. As soon as he had finished reading he picked up the phone and called the charity, despite it being Boxing Day and there being a high chance no one would answer.

The phone rang. Much to David's surprise, someone answered.

"Hello, Edinburgh Direct Aid. Dennis Rutovitz speaking."

"Hello. My name is David Headley. I read about you in the Evening News and I'd like to volunteer."

"Okay, great," Dennis responded. "Do you have a 4x4?"

David paused slightly. "No."

"Do you have the £1500 you will need to pay for costs of the trip?"

"No."

"Do you realise you will need these things to get a caravan over there?"

"Yes."

There was a pause on the other end of the phone while Dennis took in the conversation that had so far gone less than well. "How will you get them, David?" he asked.

"I don't know," David said. "But I will get them."

"Okay, well don't expect the church to help you."

The challenge was set.

"Hello Radio Forth," said the woman on the other end of the line.

"Yes, hello," David said. "I'm wondering if you can put me through to whoever deals with putting appeals out on the radio."

"Certainly sir, I'll just put you through."

Then came the holding noises. Beep beep. Beep beep. Beep beep. They were almost hypnotic.

"Hello." Finally someone had picked up again. This time it was a man.

"Hello there, my name is David Headley. I'm looking to have an appeal put out on the radio. Can you help me?"

"What is the appeal for?"

"I'd like you to put out an appeal for someone who has a 4x4 to let me borrow it and drive it to a war zone from which it may never come back. In return I will give them the use of my Ford Fiesta while I'm away, but I want it back when I return."

There was a pause of disbelief on the other end of the line. "Sure. No bother."

The appeal went out on Radio Forth the next day, broadcast all over Edinburgh and the surrounding area. After returning from Bosnia, David had begun developing something of a speaking career. He taught on homelessness at a collage in Edinburgh and also taught in churches. A couple of weekend's prior to the radio appeal he had spoken at a church in Edinburgh stressing the need for Christians to be practical in their faith. A woman who had been at the service had relayed the message to her son, a postman called Stuart.

Stuart called David after hearing the radio appeal and told him he wanted to give him his 4x4 for the trip, and that he wanted to be David's co-driver. It was agreed. The 4x4 was now in place - a 1966 Land Rover Defender - but the £1500 required still remained outstanding.

David went to his pastor. "Pastor," he said. "How would you like the opportunity to sow something beautiful into Eastern Europe?"

"You can have ten minutes on Sunday night," the pastor replied. And that was the end of the conversation.

That Sunday evening after David spoke £1700 was given in a special offering. In the days that followed a further £700 came in, which paid a large chunk of the costs for another vehicle.

The crew of people that came together to deliver the caravans were diverse to say the least. There was Dennis from Edinburgh Direct Aid - a Jewish man in his early 70s -, a squad of ex-Royal Ulster Constabulary ranking officers and two serving police officers, a joiner and a charity volunteer along with David and Stewart - the group's only Christians - and a few others. The RUC boys especially were absolutely fearless. One of them had been sitting his senior police officer exam when a gunman broke in and shot him in the back of the head. He had still lived to tell the tale and was functionally unaffected by the incident. David found the irony of the trip amusing. Here he was, a man who had served time in prison for the attempted murder of a police officer going on a huge, potentially life-threatening excursion with a bunch of police officers.

The group set off from Edinburgh castle on a Tuesday morning in January with twelve touring caravans. They were waved off by Eric Milligan who was the Mayor of Edinburgh after being interviewed by newspapers, radio stations and TV news crews and started their trip by proceeding in convoy down Edinburgh's Royal Mile, each vehicle covered with signs saying "Edinburgh to Kosovo or else!"

As they progressed down through the UK, they were joined at Liverpool by another driver, a man whose Land Rover was covered with zebra stripes, just to add an edge of subtlety.

It was cold as they travelled and the temperature seemed to drop further and further the deeper they travelled into Europe. In Switzerland the temperature dropped to -25 degrees Celsius, nearer -40 degrees with the wind chill. It was so cold that the vehicles refused to re-start after they stopped for a break and diesel was freezing in the fuel tank. The local Land Rover club in Leurich had to help them through the Brenner Pass.

They drove to Ancona in the north-east of Italy to make the final stretch of the journey across the Adriatic Sea into Kosovo. They arrived in Ancona on Sunday, six days after leaving Edinburgh. Arriving there at night they parked the caravans in what they deemed a safe and sensible place. Not long after tempers started to fray. The whole team were tired after long hours on the road, which didn't help when some of the members announced in Ancona that they would not be going into Albania because they were worried about their vehicles. Animosity arose in the group with some arguing "My nine grand Land Rover is worth as much to me as your twenty grand Land Rover is to you." The RUC officers were unimpressed as well, using the situation as an opportunity to mock. But it didn't change anything, and that meant that some people would have to make the trip over the Adriatic Sea and through Kosovo twice to ensure the delivery of the caravans.

That night many of the team had a lot to drink and went to sleep in the caravan.

A loud honking noise awoke the whole team the next morning. It sounded like a horn. David went outside his caravan to investigate, as hung-over policemen past and present poured out of their caravans in their underpants to do the same. All of a sudden everyone sprang into action and the sore heads and sleepiness disappeared. They had parked the caravans on a train track and the train was headed straight for them.

They all sprang to life and hooked up their caravans to the Land Rovers, driving them off the tracks just in time for the train to pass without hitting them. It was a close call and an interesting way to begin the next stage of their trip.

Kosovo was a grim sight. They were met at the port of Durres by streets lined with beggars, people with eye patches, others with limbs missing, children and worn and ripped clothing walking around with Kalashnikovs. The air in the place almost felt heavier and everything looked grey. People's faces were drained of colour and life.

The group were lead into an apparent 'secure compound' with the caravans while their access to the country was cleared - the process, they were told, would only take 2 hours or so. That time frame was then extended, and extended to the point where they spent three days waiting to get over the border. And it didn't matter that the compound was "secure", people still were able to climb over the walls into the compound. As the group tried to sleep in the caravans at night they were constantly being disrupted and held on edge by the sound of people moving around outside the caravans.

The facilities in the compound were another blow. They had been promised a toilet block, but found on a scouting mission to the toilet block that it in fact had no toilet in it, nor did it have any windows, sinks or running water. It was just a few walls in the shape of a toilet block which stank of urine. On one visit David was sure he saw a rat the size of a Labrador. Morale in the group was at rock bottom - they needed to use the toilet, hadn't showered and felt dirtier by the second breathing the foul, stinking air.

To make the wait bearable the group found that if they gave $10 a day to the border guards they were allowed to leave the compound on foot and walk into town. In town they rented a hotel room and told the hotel owner that no one would actually be staying in the room, but people would be coming and going frequently to use the bathroom and to take showers.

Once out of the customs compound, they drove for 30 miles by Police escort to the Police training academy in the capital city of Tirana. Driving in the city was chaos, as people drove wherever they pleased over the pot hole covered roads, paying no heed whatsoever to anyone else and refusing to move from the path of the caravan convoy.

The Police Academy looked like a fort. Officers armed with guns patrolled around the top of the walls and on the roof. It was something of a frightening prospect that even the police station had to have guards. After an overnight stay there they set off under police escort the next morning on the 140 mile drive to Kukes on the Albanian border. In the UK the trip would have taken around four hours, but the roads in Kosovo meant it took 16 hours.

There was only one road to Kukes and it wound higher and higher up the side of a mountain. There was 18 inches of snow on the ground and locals could be seen standing at the roadside shaking their heads, as if to say "there is no way you will make it."

The vehicles had to literally crawl up the hill to keep traction. With a caravan on the back and no crash barrier on the side there was nothing between them and a kilometre long drop down the mountainside. On two occasions David felt the caravan sliding.

It was only after getting to their destination and talking to UN officials that the full extent of the trouble they were in on the road was revealed. It turned out that not only were they in bandit country driving the very thing the bandits wanted, they were also being guarded by men who would in fact flee at the sight of bandits despite being armed with heavy machine guns. The guards, it turned out, were only paid around £35 per month and deemed it too small an amount of money to risk their lives for. The new found knowledge made the drive back an equally nerve wracking experience and they were glad to arrive home without incident.

Compassion fatigue set in for David when he returned from the trip. His heart was no longer in ministering to the homeless as it had been before. He had been working with homeless people and addicts for over seven years and he knew it was time to move on.

Three weeks after returning home, the situation in Kosovo got worse. It burned on David's heart to do something more about it, and he shared his desire to help the situation with an elder at church. The elder told him to get in touch with a man called Sean McNaughton who was directing outreach for the Assemblies of God in Scotland. David phoned him the next day.

The phone rang only for a short time before a man with a thick Scottish accent, tinged with the Glaswegian tendency to emphasise the end of the every sentence, answered the phone. "Hullo."

"Hello is that Sean?" David said.

"Yes it is. How can I help you?" Sean replied.

"Sean, what are you doing about Kosovo?"

"Nothing. We have an existing project in Ukraine that is taking our resources."

"Okay, "David said, his mere tone giving away the fact that he was dissatisfied with the answer and was about to add something else. "If you had £100,000 would you do something about it?"

"Yes," said Sean.

"Good," David replied. He hung up the phone.

Two days later Sean called David. David picked up the phone.

"Hello," he said.

"Where is my £100,000?" Sean cut in, without even so much as a hello.

"I'm still praying for it!" David answered.

The conversation ended there and the men hung up. It was blunt, but to the point.

It weighed on David that he had effectively promised funds for a humanitarian effort he had had no means of supplying them. Later that day he was in conversation with a neighbour who had just returned from doing her shopping at the supermarket. In the midst of the conversation she said "I noticed there are a lot of items that are buy one, get one free. They should make it 'Buy one, send one to Kosovo." Just then something in David's spirit clicked.

He went back into his house and got on the phone to the local Safeway's manager. "What are you doing about Kosovo?" he asked.

The manager gave him a response about what Safeway as an organisation were doing. It was a default answer that didn't satisfy David.

"It's not enough," David said.

After some deliberation the store manager invited David into the store that Saturday to hold an appeal. It was an offer he wasn't about to turn down.

He arrived at the Safeway on Saturday with a crew of people made up of friends from work, from church and wherever else he could muster them. With them they had hundreds of leaflets asking people to consider buying items from a list to send to Kosovo and also to make a donation towards the carriage of the gifts to Kosovo.

At the end of the day they had £20,000 of groceries and had gathered ten times more money than any other appeal had ever received in that supermarket. The store manager was so impressed with the success of the appeal that he called every other store manager in Edinburgh telling them to have David and his team in to do an appeal in store as soon as possible. At first David was blown away by the kindness and support that the manager was showing to their campaign, until he realised that the store's earning targets had been greatly exceeded thanks to their campaign and it was therefore financially in the interest of Safeway to have them there!

The following Monday David went into work and asked for 60 days unpaid leave so he could really throw himself behind the mission of humanitarian aid. He had no idea how he would pay his mortgage and feed his three kids but he believed God was behind the work and that He would provide.

He never went back to work with the Church of Scotland and he went on to live without a salary for many years campaigning for, raising and delivering aid to Albania, Kosovo, Macedonia and many other countries. It was at times embarrassing how generous God was to him, but other times God chose to provide at the eleventh hour. Faith became real when there was nothing else but faith to rely on. Faith became real when it was the only justification for living life that way, for forsaking the comforts of this world for the knowledge that there is something bigger and better than what the world we see before us offers and that something is Jesus Christ. It wasn't simply a faith in nothing, or even a faith that things would work out fine. The faith that David was living was one that was based on a revelation of who God is. The money to pay the bills was provided in miraculous ways by a God he believed in and personally knew not some far off being that may or may not exist.

This man who as a child ran riot, as a teenager caused even more trouble, as a young man was imprisoned for theft and attempted murder and then met God in prison had been changed so completely that it was as if he were a completely new man.

PROLOGUE

By David Headley

So why did I decide this story was worth writing? I guess the answer is fourfold.

Primarily, because I want to be a witness to how God has completely changed my life. He is real and promises to be found by the earnest seeker. Do you believe it might be possible to know the living God? Do you believe He actually might want YOU to know Him? Imagine if I am right. Imagine if you are minding your own business and struggling along with life or busy with working hard at school. Climbing the career ladder or just being mum. Day goes into day, week into week and year into year. Sadly the day to consider what it's all about may never ever arrive. THIS MIGHT BE THE MOMENT FOR YOU NOW!

I believe God is badly represented by me and many other Christians. I believe He is above all so so merciful. He is solid, not changing His mind or being driven by human emotion. He loves each of us as if we were the only person on the planet. I believe He was there when that horrible thing happened to you willing you to cry out to Him. I believe even today years afterwards He wants to heal you and help you reach your full potential. GOD IS FOR YOU! Oh do not misunderstand me, He is not celebrating those bad or even evil decisions you might have made, but today is the day of mercy. Admit them, get real and stop pretending all is well. Why not, for one second, humble yourself. Admit you do not know it all. It is cool to have many questions - you don't need to know it all. However, stop right now whether you are in the bath, on a train or in a library. Why not say my prayer; "God if you are real, please reveal yourself to me. I want to live as you planned me to. I want your purposes for my life." Out loud is great, in your head if you are embarrassed in a public place. Say it, mean it and begin the adventure of your life.

Secondly, I meet so many Christians today who have written people off. They have no belief that God could or wanted to change them. They spent huge amounts of time telling you how bad the people were or how they did this or that, but spent little or no time praying for God to intervene.

The Bible tells us that God uses the foolish things of the world to dumbfound the wise. Yet so much of Christendom today is chasing education or the perfect sermon. Please do not misunderstand me, I am so grateful for the scholars I have met who helped shape my life, but the answers I believe are found in God, not study. While in prison an Elim minister faithfully taught me New Testament Greek on a bi-weekly basis. He was a brilliant man who loved Jesus and was driven in his Hebrew and Greek studies not to gain qualifications but to draw closer to Jesus.

I wonder how our neighbourhoods would change if we asked for God's heart for the hurting and the lost. Any fool can judge! I often found in my time working with people with addictions that they had opinions about EVERYTHING and often excuses for EVERYTHING too. So next time you see a hopeless case, please do not judge but seek God. Pray like there is no tomorrow. Reach out and act in faith not fear. My God is a God of miracles yesterday, today and forever. You might begin to be a part of a truly amazing adventure.

Thirdly, Although God has changed me so I am unrecognisable, I still might throw something at the next Christian who says we shouldn't feed the hungry, or cloth the naked or practically demonstrate our faith. Jesus tells many stories about people who are happy to preach but not to care. They are bad witnesses and could be sued for misrepresenting God. The God I know and love says that He knows how many hairs are on your head. Wow, now what is what I call detail!

Christian, if your heart isn't broken when you hear of people in need, maybe your rebirth had complications. If you have no desire to see the hungry fed, clothed and housed are you really representing God or giving yourself an excuse not to give. It is NOT evangelism or aid. It is both. Aid without evangelism isn't that smart. Evangelism without aid in places where people are hungry or homeless is offensive. We found as we began caring in crisis zones that people begged us to tell them why we were there. We did not seek a pulpit or recognition but just believed that it was God's will that we would DEMONSTRATE His care. I have decided not to share how many people came to faith through this work in case another formula is created. However this work was, and still is very fruitful.

A life spent in a relationship with God IS the most amazing adventure of your life. Life before Jesus for me was one of sowing destruction everywhere I went. It was all about me and my needs, never giving a thought for anybody else. My word focused around me and mine.

Since becoming a Christian? I have travelled to thirty nine different countries and shared my faith in places as diverse as the mountains of Nepal and Kosovo and the streets of Albania. I have had my heart broken by orphans who lived on the street in Tirana calling me daddy. I've been blessed to share meals with people who have seen their family executed and yet they declare that Jesus has given them the power to forgive the executors. I have heard a girl who was raped nearly a thousand times say "I am so happy because through this I came to the end of my strength and found Jesus." I gave away a life of misery and shame and was given, in exchange, a most amazing adventure.

I go out of my door in the morning and wonder who God will have me speak to that day. I often find he leads me to hurting people, people having a bad day or just people He wants to tell of His great love. I have flown a plane, driven super cars, captained a power boat round Scotland, been in two war zones and dined with many famous people. What an exciting life...... but be under no illusion, all this is completely second rate to sitting in the presence of God and knowing that He loves me beyond my wildest dreams.

Did you choose life? Will you choose life in all its fullness?

Published by 1st Choice Christian Publishing